The
Land
is HOLY

The Land is HOLY

noam keim

ISBN 978-1-7377184-8-2
Library of Congress Control Number: 2023951546

Editor
Meher Manda

Interior Layout and Design
Lantz Arroyo

Jacket Design and Interior Illustrations
Nicholas Hurd

Printed and published in Brooklyn, New York by Radix.

Radix Printing & Publishing Cooperative
522 Bergen Street
Brooklyn, New York 11217

radix.coop

This collection is the winner of the 2023 Megaphone Prize, an annual contest dedicated to the discovery of urgent and interrogative works from debut writers of color. Special thanks to our guest judge, Hanif Abdurraqib.

For more information on the prize, see **radix.coop/megaphone-prize**.

Advanced Praise for *The Land is Holy*

"*The Land is Holy* is a collection overrun with generosity—one that generously asks a reader to consider what they might have taken for granted, what they might still be taking for granted. The stillness and beauty that not only surrounds us, but informs the history of what came before us. An understanding of what has been painted over, repurposed, and colonized, and how freedom can still be found, despite."

—Hanif Abdurraqib,
They Can't Kill Us Until They Kill Us

"Lush and lyrical, powerfully evocative and intellectually trenchant, *The Land is Holy* is the shimmering debut collection of an essayist of rare talent."

—Kai Cheng Thom,
Falling Back In Love With Being Human

"*The Land is Holy* is a gift. There is so much wisdom in these pages—sentences that sway with music and lyricism, an essayist moving through the world with an open heart, with curiosity and generosity. Every page teaches us something about what it means to be connected to a people, what it means to be human, and alive."

—Jaquira Díaz,
Ordinary Girls

"A dazzling debut that challenges readers to imagine who and what was on the land before us so that we can be better stewards for possibilities."

—Grace Talusan,
The Body Papers

"A must-read for those on a quest for ancestral re-membrance, liberatory healing and meaningful possibilities of redemption within the wreckage of our colonized world."

—Layla K. Feghali,
The Land In Our Bone

"An American soldier fucked a Vietnamese farmgirl. Thus my mother exists. / Thus I exist. Thus no bombs = no family = no me."

—Ocean Vuong, "Notebook Fragments"

"Our land is holy, our land is history."

—Belly ft. M.I.A., Meek Mill, "Immigrant"

* * *

To David "Dawud" Lee, who I have loved imperfectly and will forever mourn.

Table of Contents

A Life in Flight

A STORK FLIES WESTWARD ACROSS THE FAINT BLUE LINE OF the Vosges Mountains, over vineyards, coming back to the nests of her Alsatian villages. In the distance, she can see the village of half-timbered walls and roofs of flat clay tiles. Her long black and white wings streak the clouds with their fluttering. Soon, she'll be back, perched on the top of the church. Home for the spring.

* * *

In July 1985, a large commercial El-Al plane, white with light dark blue letters, lands on the tarmac of the international Mulhouse-Freiburg-Basel Euroairport. It is a hot and humid day in the Dreieckland. A woman holding a baby in her arms walks down the steps. Olive skin, hair cropped short, she is wearing a dress striped of white and red, wrinkled by the seat and the movement of children on her lap. Holding her left hand, a toddler with short curly hair waddles down the stairs. She is meeting her husband at the arrival gate. They haven't seen each other in six months, and the international calls can only last so long. Hassida smiles under the summer sky of her new home.

* * *

Every year, when the weather gets colder, when the days grow shorter, storks migrate from their European spring and summer homes to the warmth of southern lands. Some will fly above the Gibraltar strait before continuing their journey towards West Africa. Others will fly around the Mediterranean and above the Levant, before finding their way to the savannah. The storks will fly two-thousand miles to their winter abodes, completing their southward route in a few weeks only. They will leave their nests, built on roofs and trees to find the sun, returning only when the threat of cold has evaporated. They will return. Storks always find their way back home.

* * *

I was born on Christmas Day in the desert of Palestine, the settler child of Fernand and Hassida who gave me two names for my two lineages. Noam Andrée. In Hebrew נֹעַם means beautiful. Proverbs 3:17. *Her ways are pleasant ways, and all her paths, peaceful.* In French, Andrée is the feminized version of my grandfather's name. My father, too, was named after his grandfather; my mother named after her grandmother. All three of us named in the tradition of our people, a tradition meant to help us find our way home.

* * *

In the new apartment on rue du Sauvage, at the center of a city she doesn't understand, Hassida tries to teach her children about the way of their line, with the ingredients of new worlds. Everything here is different, nothing feels familiar anymore. The sand of her childhood is replaced with the cobblestone streets of Mulhouse. In this new city she lives above a store that isn't the makolet of her youth. The milk here is sold in bottles, the stores are brightly lit and haggling is a faux-pas. She buys her groceries in a Monoprix, adapting to the new foods and flavors. She's a French citizen now. On the food packaging, on the walls of the city, storks pictures, the symbol of this new region. Alsace.

Bonjour, j'peux vous aider? The sounds Hassida's throat has adapted to make in her youth are not the sounds her husband's mouth makes anymore. No longer the foreigner she met in her desert home, Fernand has adapted back to the climate of his childhood home. Fernand's throat creates heavily Germanic sounds now, sounds they have never shared before. *Wie gehts?* Who is the man she married? Was the version of him she knew only an adaptation to a new environment? She is the foreigner now, living in a world that only he knows.

On the streets, Hassida often hears the language of her parents, guttural and holy, but those aren't her people. In the Zionist State, she was taught to fear other Arab bodies. In this cacophony of foreign and familiar sounds, Hassida isn't home anymore. Only connected to her ancestral lands by the name given to her by her mother, and the body of her children. Her children whose mouths are betraying the home they were born into, their tongues and bodies moving between languages without effort.

* * *

Storks have circled human civilizations for long enough to be embedded in our common mythology. Divine creatures. Jews and Muslims alike are forbidden by their holy scriptures to eat the flesh of the stork. Every year, in the fall, our people observed the large white birds leave in flocks and disappear for a few months, only to return, as the Earth warmed again, to the same exact land. Reentering the nests they left behind. Magical beings embodying the spirals of time.

Lek-Lek, the swishing sound of the stork's wings flapping in concert. Her throat creates a cackle that roars through the sky. She will settle in Poland and Germany, but in France, the stork nests only in the far-eastern parts of the hexagon. Her habit of always returning has given her the aura of a good omen. Wherever she builds her home, whoever's house she chooses will be blessed with abundant crops and good health.

* * *

Sometime in the year 1955, somewhere in the Naqab desert of Palestine, Zohara Chouraqui, born Assouline, dreams about her mother. Zohara is pregnant again, and she has been waiting for ancestral kin to visit her and tell her about the child to be. Whoever comes, will gift their name to this new member of the family. Zohara hasn't seen her mother in a long time, and her body relaxes in her maternal presence. Only twenty years old, Zohara wishes she could be a child for a moment; she tells her mother about this new life they are building away from home. Zohara tries to tell her own mother about the ways her body is shifting in this new environment, she tells her about her first-born daughter. She tells her about the burgeoning colonial project, how she's surrounded by Jews from all over the world. In the vision her sleeping body has created, Zohara and her mother are still in Marrakech, and as Zohara dreams so does the baby growing inside of her. Together, they all walk through the mellah, together they wail. "I have missed you, Um." Zohara's mother reminds her: our people are our home, our elders are our home, never sever the roots. Zohara understands what her mother asks her to do. Zohara will name her daughter Hassiba, a name that reminds her mouth of the warmth of her mother's womb.

* * *

In Ancient Egypt, the death of the body was believed to only be a milestone in an intricate understanding of life and the soul. The dead body would be preserved, and the mouth opened, for the ba, or mobile spirit to be released into a potential eternal life.

In their hieroglyph system, they would draw the ba as a human-headed stork, mimicking the movement of the soul leaving the body to have a life of its own. Spending days amongst the living, and nights across realms. With her wings, the ba could move through worlds, connecting to the Gods and the underworld. Souls no longer tethered by human bodies, moving through generations and always coming back, circling between two worlds.

* * *

On a Shabbat day of February 1956, Zohara pushes one more time before she hears the wail of life. Hassiba is born, in a cloud of health and bones. Exhausted and relieved, Zohara can breathe again. Her daughter is alive, and with her continues the line. Child of Zohara, grandchild of Hassiba. Spiraling of time.

* * *

In Kaliningrad, scientists raise storks without their mothers, away from their flock. In the aviary, they nurture their young birds who can help them answer the question: Can the storks find their way to their ancestral land on their own? Do they carry the map to home within their blood or is it a lesson taught?

The scientists release the birds, equipped with technology allowing them to follow the trip. They learn that the storks know the general direction of home. In flocks, they fly south to the sun, their blood the compass guiding their imprecise journey. The storks won't quite make it home, often missing their place of birth by a few miles, but they will be close to their ancestral lands, at last. During the journey, though, some will perish in their disorientation, failing to find the food and water necessary to sustain themselves on their way home.

* * *

In the fall of 2021, I wake up in my home on Turtle Island. The clock reads 3 A.M., and in my dreams I run away from disaster, carrying only the objects in my pack. Climate collapse and ancestral trauma are colliding again. Almost ten years after I escaped, I have found myself called to do ancestral work, awakened by the constant thug inside of my chest, that whispers the answer to my hopelessness is within my roots. I have been spending months trying to unearth my family's lineages, even after I broke free from their lines. I haven't felt satiated from the plants and dreams and psychics I consulted but they are all I have. My blood is trying to tell me something, and in the dark of the house I am trying to listen.

Slowly, I open the covers, trying not to stir Johnny sleeping soundly. Mimi the cat wakes up, startled by the darkness that envelopes us. Together we walk downstairs. Half a cup of kibble, tea in the kettle. In the thick of the night, we settle on the couch. I open my computer while she curls up against my hip. My blood hums: *our people are our home, our elders are our home.* I start to build a virtual family tree to help me reconnect to the sounds and places of the people who have made me. One name at a time, I unravel the spool left by my elders. I dig into my veins for the compass of our traditions, even those I have foregone. In my quest for freedom and safety, I have lost my way home, and I am trying to learn which way it is again.

* * *

One day, between February 1956 and 1984, Hassiba Chouraqui becomes Hassida Chouraqui. It is unclear when Hassiba decides to change the ancestral name given to her after the dream. We could speculate that she imagined her new name an adaptation to the Zionist State that became her land. Maybe she was ready to close the hole at the center of her or maybe she wanted to sever the thread to her ancestral land. There are many reasons one might change their name, but in the tradition of our people it is a desecration. We might be generous and imagine she uncovered a grand maternal treason. Regardless, she replaces the bet with a dalet. One letter changing her destiny. Hassiba became Hassida. Hassida, the Hebrew word for stork, becoming the only home she would know. In between worlds, across seas, forever circling never quite being able to land between her two homes.

* * *

In the winter of 1992, I am sitting in the kitchen with my mother and her sister. They are separated by twelve years but share colors and bone structure. They laugh. Around the table we are settled in our chairs, eating olives and spitting their core on small dishes brought from Occupied Palestine. We are speaking Hebrew to each other, in the close intimacy of our shared throats. My mother's sister is visiting; she has settled a few hundred miles away from us, the only sibling close enough to see regularly. In a defiant gesture, she calls my mother the name of their grandmother, the first time I hear that word. "Hassiba," she says, and my mother's body tenses up in anger, her arm hits her sibling with a rag. A dark cloud hovers over the room and when the thickness dissipates, the scene is never spoken of again.

* * *

The stork is at the end of her life voyage. She has taught her fledgling everything they need for the frost to come. Together, as part of their home flock, they will fly south like all generations before them. They will not doubt their task, the movement is required for their survival and they learn that so is life. Half of the year spent in the savannah, half of the year spent near the hops and grapevines. In each home, they find a part of themselves they have left behind a season past.

The Earth is warming, and the storks shave a few miles off each trip south. The ancestral lands that fed them have been replaced by cities and fields of tainted seeds. Their voyages become more difficult. Soon they only go as far as the edge of the continent. No more Gibraltar strait, they will rest in Portugal, like the flock of humans also avoiding the snow. The stork is at the end of her life voyage, she can only hope they will always find their way to their shifting home, the place that ties them to their lineage's past, the tree where they had gathered materials and nested, the water source that kept them alive. She can only hope that they will keep her memory alive in the paths they travel and in the choices they make. After all, home has always been whatever they make out of their circumstances.

* * *

In the dark of my home, I type furiously. Clack, clack, clack. I uncover too many ancestral lands to carry with me. Many names, many places, never enough details to tell the stories my elders never taught me. In the dark of my home, sitting on my couch with my cat curled up against me, I wonder what my mother left of herself when she turned herself into a bird. I wonder if this is when she lost her way home, digging the hole in her body she would fill with anger that would terrorize her children.

And I wonder about me, her child, who circled the Earth a few times now, moving from land to land, further and further away from her. The child who disappeared, who made a home in a place without ancestral ties, who decided to end the line with their body. What of this child did I have to leave behind? In the thick of the night, no matter how long it has been since I have spoken to her, I seem to always return to the feeling of being my mother's child. In the thick of the night, I stay small, terrorized, unable to quite taste this freedom I created for myself, my mouth, instead, filled with the grief of exile, never knowing which way to look for home.

The Mallards

"I N MY NEXT LIFE, I'LL COME BACK AS A BIRD AND SHIT ON everybody who was mean to me," he tells me before erupting in rapacious laughter. I draw the image for him with a purple marker and we laugh. A beak, wings, and three dots falling from the sky tell the new ending to his story. It is a slow morning in Philadelphia, and we are watching a documentary narrated by David Attenborough, marveling at the ways birds create daily miracles. Sitting in a somewhat sterile room that I have decorated the best way I could, we create laughter out of the dances of birds of paradise and the fantasies of new lives.

Kai understands a bird as a metaphor for the freedom that was never granted to him in this lifetime. A lifetime of institutions bearing different names but creating the same conditions: prisons, foster homes, hospitals, psychiatric institutions. Spaces of confinement and dehumanization. I understand that the birds we watch on the screen offer us a way to develop hope, possibility, resilience. Kai thinks about the next life, and the ways he'll enact vengeance on every system that destroyed him. We make a good pair.

Kai comes to see me every day of the week, so that we can work on some of the challenges life on the outside poses to him. In my office, we often reach the limits of this conditional freedom he is now experiencing, conditional because of rules imposed by the State, conditional because there was never enough safety, belonging, and dignity for his mind to adapt to this new life. On the days we meet in my office, we take short, deliberate walks past the crane erected in the middle of the construction site across the street. He dreams of climbing the narrow stairs, he dreams of seeing the city from above our heads. I get dizzy thinking about the heights.

* * *

"I want to tell stories of the people I work with because there is so much to learn from these narratives."

In a conversation circle of social workers, that could have been any circle really, an argument that feels familiar unfolds, the endless question of care work. How much do you get to learn from someone else's life without building a relationship with them? In this circle, debating the righteousness of telling stories of others, tortured by the state, I dissociate and dream of islands of secrets and infinite freedom.

* * *

One of the many things you should know about birdwatching – or birding – is that it isn't just the activity of watching birds. Birding is an industry, centered around the accumulation of encounters with birds. Every state park or national one will give you a list with boxes to tick. Bird names organized by type in neat lists for you to peruse quickly. An inventory of sorts helping the accumulation of labels. As if you could possess birds by ticking the box next to their name.

The second thing you might want to know about birdwatching is that it's a forty-one billion dollar industry. Sometimes it's expensive gear like oversized lenses for cameras that you'll use to capture birds, sometimes it's the trips to exotic spaces to see one specific bird. American birdwatchers spend up to twenty billion dollars a year in travel, bird seeds and birding paraphernalia: binoculars, cameras and lenses, hats and hiking shoes. Granted there are forty-five million birders in America but the scale of the numbers makes me dizzy.

One more thing: a lot of birders think of themselves as doing conservationist work, helping save an environment, rather than just ticking boxes. And many of them are right, while others consume nature like any other hobby.

* * *

I have tried to be a birder before.

In September 2015, the Pope came to Philadelphia for a few days and turned the streets into chaos. Parts of the city were enclosed into safety zones with police and army patrolling the area, to allow for the large numbers of Catholic pilgrims. For the time of this visit, all of us who lived on the Western side of the river were stuck in our neighborhood. That weekend of the Pope's visit, I was supposed to see my friend Jo and whatever plans we had made were derailed by the spectacle of papal security.

Jo and I had met while I volunteered my working days for the local Books Through Bars chapter. There, I used the skills I had accumulated over the years working in French libraries, bookstores, and publishing companies in Mulhouse, Montreal, Paris, and San Francisco. I sorted and organized. I packed orders. I read hundreds if not thousands of letters from people incarcerated in Pennsylvania, Maryland, New Jersey and Virginia who described their desperation, disconnection and desire to access new worlds through the act of reading. Jo was another volunteer there, and we struck a friendship, one of the first tangible ones in this new city. In this relationship, I learned that Americans love activities and that the long hours of my teens and twenties spent in coffee shops just talking didn't always appeal to the American mind. That weekend, as we tried to find an activity on our side of the city, we found a listing for a guided walk, a birdwatching tour. Neither one of us had ever done it, but I was still so painfully new to living full-time in the US that I would have done anything to experience grounding, belonging, safety.

* * *

What stories do we get to hear?
Which ones aren't ours to share?
How many details do we need to tell our traumas?
What is the line between accumulation and compassion?

Over the years, I have asked myself these questions repeatedly, as I deepen my relationship with trauma work. As I listen to people whose sovereignty over their stories has been taken away by systems. How do I tell you stories that make sense without the context in which they unfolded?

*   *   *

I was a birder before I named myself one.

For my tenth birthday, I asked my father for the best gift he could ever buy me: a telescope. I would drag the instrument made to watch the stars to the more prosaic banks of our town's river and stand on the side, telescope angled towards the water. Silently, I would watch mallards, animals I already knew so well, observing the many details of their feathers, body. I would stand mesmerized by the shimmer of the dark green heads of the males, the hidden patches of blue that would reveal themselves with the fluttering of wings, the stripes of brown on a female's head that looked like delicate brush strokes. I would watch them swim together and find pleasure in the prolonged relationship, imagining myself gliding on the water, untethered by human needs.

It was the year after I had been raped, and there wasn't room in our house for me to talk about the nightmares that had intensified, and the alienation that had taken over. In the silence of others, I learned to turn healing inwards.

On the day the catastrophic loss of safety and agency happened, I blurted the truth to my father, not because I wanted to, but because my body couldn't keep them in. Days later, I would try to sneak out of the house before the police came for my deposition but failed. I sat in our living room surrounded by adults who forced every detail out of me, until they were satisfied. I knew they were doing so to protect me, but on that day, another part of my childhood disappeared, another part of me was killed. Not the same part as the one that was wounded during the assault on my body. It was something else, another tear in my own sense of safety, the knowledge that nothing of mine could remain mine alone, that everything of mine would be forced to be shared. That day, I became aware of a necessary disconnection from my inner self. That day I went back to school and told my classmates

I had been at the doctor's. I told them that after the appointment my mother had taken me to McDonalds. It was all part of a lie I needed to tell to stay alive.

On the river banks, the telescope allowed me to experience the world from a distance. One eye against the lens, I would focus my energy and attention to a small portion of what had become a terrifying environment. If I observed only small vignettes of it, portions that felt calming and reassuring, maybe I would be able to heal. If I could stay in the silence and control how much I experienced at once, maybe I would be able to reconnect with a sense of safety. A lonely and silent practice of looking at the feathers of a beloved animal until the world fell back into place. Letting my eyes linger on the green collar, the beak. I already knew what the bird would look like, but with my telescope, I could deepen my sense of its colors, textures, body creating ripples in the water. There's a simplicity in watching a bird, a simplicity that hides webs of complex relationships that define the world. The plants that surround the swimming mallard, the insects flying, the ways males and females communicate with each other. On the banks of the river, as I observed their world, I rebuilt myself.

A decade later, this time coming back from a month-long stay in a psychiatric hospital, I went back to the river banks. The telescope had gathered too much dust, but I could still spend time in the quiet company of shimmery green old friends.

One mallard. Two mallards. Three mallards.

* * *

Birds are one of the few species that have thoroughly found ways to live in the bleak ecosystem of cities. Storks, sparrows, swallows, pigeons and mallards were some of my first loves, miraculous reminders of the city of my youth. Lessons in adaptation.

My first American birdwatching expedition with Jo was a short trolley jaunt to southwest Philadelphia at the John Heinz National Wildlife Refuge at Tinicum, the first urban refuge of its kind. A protected network of marshes, forests, and meadows organized around a lake, now swallowed by the city. Train tracks and roads surround it and the airport towers are visible from the trails, but the birds remain.

On this first birdwatching expedition we walked the mile or so from the trolley to the park and checked in at the front desk: the attendant handed us binoculars we could borrow and directed us to our guide, a ranger surrounded by older people wearing the same shades of khaki. September was beautiful that day.

* * *

On an early fall day, I am sitting in a prison yard with my friend Habib, surrounded by forests of the Anthracite country of Pennsylvania. We drove for a few hours through the mountains and the confederate flags to get here. The prison is on top of a mountain and the tree greens are shining against the blinding blue of the sunny sky. We wouldn't know that, from where we are sitting: a picnic table in an austere yard surrounded by walls so tall that all we can see is a small square of sky.

It is a rare treat to sit outside during a prison visit, as we are usually forced to sit side by side on uncomfortable plastic chairs facing the vending machines and tiny windows placed up high. Today the room is full of families and friends, and the whispers accumulate to a fantastic roar. Emboldened by the sun, we asked for permission to be outside and were granted the opportunity when a table opened up. In the courtyard, we sit at a big table, one of four, as an armed guard slowly circles the slab of concrete, weapons in sight. We're not allowed to touch each other, and between us sit trays filled with overpriced chips, chocolate bars and popcorn.

This is what you get when you try to maintain a relationship with someone you love who is deemed by the state to be dangerous: a few hours of naked talk as prison guards observe your every move. No gifts, no outside interventions. Just you and them and your money in vending machines until you feel full of sugar and carbs that will sit in your belly on the drive back reminding you of all the ways the state wounds your body.

In the courtyard we catch up, we talk about liberation, we create small rituals. We're discussing a mutual friend's release from prison when a starling flies above us. One of my favorites, a mundane bird that has invaded American cities. I have a tattoo of a starling on my left arm but the tattoo doesn't convey their beauty, the ink incapable of reproducing the miraculous shimmer of green and purple hidden in their wings. Habib has never seen this tattoo because in order to enter a prison I have to cover my body more than I would in the streets. My outfits are austere and ill-fitting to make the security pat downs easier. In the yard, emboldened by the starling's apparition, I lift the sleeve of my shirt just a little bit as the guard turns around to show the bird on my tricep.

"A starling," I exclaim before the bird disappears behind the walls away from the minuscule slice of sky that we can see. For a second, in the apparition I experience glee before returning to the necessary disconnection required by our location. Habib doesn't know the starling, because he does not have access to the sky as often as I do, he does not have access to the sky because he has spent the entirety of my existence on this Earth behind these walls. The invasive bird brought in from Europe is not one that he is familiar with, another symbol of worlds lost.

* * *

Over the years Jo and I spend a lot of our weekends armed with binoculars, walking amongst groups of birders, as we call them. Often the only people perceived as women, mostly the only queers, we stand out with our cutoffs and baseball caps and colorful outfits in seas of olive and beige purchased at REI and LL Bean. We listen to men teach us lessons we never requested and use that energy to receive information we are trying to glean. We brandish our binoculars towards branches and brambles and trees, hoping to see enough of a bopping body to identify and check the box. We have the enthusiasm and naïveté of beginners and our odd duo elicits the condescension and amusement that I have become accustomed to.

We are birders now. Birders as in people who like to invest time and money and energy chasing after animals whose entire life is built around not being seen. Birders, as in people who like to accumulate name after name, until they have seen them all. I do not understand this impulse, I do not understand what makes someone want to tick boxes instead of watching the bird who wants to be seen, the ones in the ecosystem we know, and to deepen that bond. I do not understand what makes somebody want to capture a rare sight, instead of deepening what is already familiar.

Birders know that catching a glimpse of a red-breasted nuthatch requires them to sit as still as possible, and to blend within the environment they inhabit. Sometimes I feel like the bird, sometimes I feel like the man preparing the humongous lens for the picture.

* * *

Is this when I tell you that even when I was nine years old, I didn't want him to go to a prison? That he raped me while engaged to be married? That he was teaching me how to play the saxophone and how to breathe? That I can still feel the roughness of the blanket he asked me to put over my head? Is this when I mention the mental health treatment he received instead? That I don't really know what happened to him after that, but that I have always wished him healing?

Sometimes, I regret not having as much empathy for myself as I did for him. In the alternate reality of my life, I would have told my father what happened and my parents would have embraced me and told me there wasn't anything I did that would make an adult man think he was in love with a child. We would have cried together and grieved. Individually, they would take me out and ask me how I was doing. They would come to my room at night, just to remind me of the safety of their body. In that other life I could have lived, my shame would have been healed with others entrusted with my care. I would tell my friends in school, and they too would say "I am sorry and I love you," holding the sacredness of the story told in confidence. In this other reality, sharing my story would be met with genuine compassion, instead of flattening and projections. In this other reality I would feel empowered to share my trauma with you rather than exposed.

Maybe then, I would only look at the mallards for the thrill of the encounter.

* * *

I am not a birder anymore. I have let my binoculars and identification books accumulate dust in abandoned corners of my house. At some point, I realized I couldn't quite be what was expected of the habit. I couldn't learn all the names and identifiers, count my way through the sky. I couldn't find joy in the fleeting encounters, and the identification based on details gleaned from a distance. What I wanted of birds is what I wanted as a child on the banks of the river: a relationship of safety, belonging, and dignity, a deep and slow relationship built on the trust of complexity.

I still walk around the lake of the John Heinz refuge, and I still point at familiar sights. A finch, a robin, a woodpecker, a catbird. I often misname the bird in front of me, confusing them for another avian creature. But I recognize their wings and feathers. Sometimes. And I exclaim with glee at the sight of a starling on my street.

I am not a birder anymore, even if sometimes, the impulse to own, to accumulate, to check the box is too strong to avoid. I have returned to the 10-year old version of myself, silently observing and deepening the bonds with the world around me, finding healing in the sustained connections with the familiar. I have returned to youthful wisdom and shifted the ways I understand secrets and stories. Now the recipient of so many, I hold their precious weight in my hand, practicing dignity and belonging: "I am sorry and I love you," the promise spoken or not of never-ending secrecy. Together, building a bond that reverberates safety, helping to rewrite histories.

The Aoudads

WHEN I THINK ABOUT HOME, I THINK ABOUT MARRAKECH, a place I have only been to once, as part of an ill-planned family vacation with my parents and younger sibling in 1999. I don't think about my current house to which I own a deed, the many apartments I rented over the years or the one I was raised in. When I think about Marrakech, I don't think about the terrible all-inclusive hotel we stayed in, or the scams my parents kept falling for. I don't think about the shame I felt walking with them, crude and isolated from every other family in the hotel who was having a good time, while we ate our dinners in silence. I think about the mellah of my grandparents' childhood, a place that only lives in the memory of the dead.

Safta Zohara and Saba Eliyahu told me and the rest of the family that their love story started in childhood. They told us that they had to leave so that they could be together, and that it was the reason why they left Morocco in the late 1940s. The love alone was meant to explain leaving families behind, transiting through Marseille and a refugee camp in the Zionist State. Their love alone explained a life built on the desert that was home to other people, away from the imperial city of their childhood and the grave of their beloved ancestors.

Safta Zohara and Saba Eliyahu are both dead now, and my mother and my father might as well be, so all that is left for me is genealogy websites, history books, psychics, and my imagination. It isn't much, but it is the way I try to tell myself the story of a home abandoned. It is the way I get to explain the tears that come up when I hear Arabic, the comfort of sand under my bare feet, and my affinity for mint, rue, rosemary, rose, and wormwood.

I know that Safta Zohara and Saba Eliyahu flattened their story to make it palatable. I know that they were both part of a moment in history when Arab Jews were manipulated to leave their homelands to populate the lower echelons of the Zionist State and justify the rejection of Arabness as a whole. I know that, because their story of migration is the story of thousands of people, the books and websites have taught me.

* * *

In 1957, a year after my mother was born in the Occupied Naqab city, where her parents were placed by the Zionist authorities, a city currently known as Beer-Sheva, Texas wildlife officials released about forty aoudads in the Palo Duro Canyon to offer hunting opportunities to ranchers. In English, the aoudad is also called the Barbary sheep, as in the sheep from the Barbary Coast, the 15th century term that describes the North African littoral west of Egypt. As in the coast of Morocco, Algeria, Tunisia, Libya; as in what my people have known as al-Maghrib, the Maghreb, the West.

The first record of an aoudad on the American continent dates to a zoo in Jersey in 1900. They brought them by boats, from the ports of Africa to the coasts of Turtle Island. Mountain goats extracted from the deserts where they thrived in spaces that look impossible to the human eye to be placed behind the protection of fences, to be observed and enjoyed by the crowds of the Eastern seaboard.

I wonder if, in the zoo of Jersey in 1900, they built structures that resembled the rocks aoudads climbed in their home landscape. I wonder if, in the zoo of Jersey, they marveled at how little water they needed to survive. As the aoudads settled in their new artificial habitat, their numbers grew too fast for the zoos to keep up with the new generations of desert sheep.

So, when the longhorn population dwindled in the American West because their habitat was being decimated, it made sense to replace them with their North African cousins, who bred so fast that not even the ferocity of Texan hunters could eradicate them. As if their lives could just be swapped without any consequences. As if introducing the aoudads to the American West could negate the destruction already underway. Just like that, they plopped Barbary sheep in a canyon of the American West, hoping that they would adapt, like they did in the zoo in Jersey and the other enclosed environments in which they had thrived before. They did thrive, adapting so well that they became part of the thread of destruction, displacing the remaining longhorns and a multitude of plants and smaller members of the Texan ecosystems. The aoudads followed the rules of the land they were asked to live on.

I first heard about the aoudads of Texas on a winter day of the pandemic on the archeological site of the Hueco Tanks, a 40-minute drive from the city of El Paso. It was my last day in the Chihuahuan desert, and Johnny and I were stopping into the park before heading back East to our jobs and life and house. We had scheduled the pictograph tour with a phone call the week before, as we sat on a bench, watching the cars drive through the bridge to Juarez. Hundreds of people, leaving the American West, crossing a militarized border to go home daily.

We didn't know what to expect of the pictograph tour, we just knew that the site was sacred to the Mescalero Apache and Tigüa people and that it was recommended on every tourist list we had read. We also knew that the tour was our only way to get inside the park, and that we were lucky to get a spot so soon; we learned that people schedule time in the park months in advance.

Johnny and I were on a month-long vacation, meant to help us rebuild from the burn out that was eating away at us. After two years of pandemic, two years of trying to keep people alive and out of prisons, we had lost connection to each other. We were spending our days in meetings, tending to crises that left us too depleted to care for each other anymore. Around us, everybody was breaking up and it was feeling like our turn. We thought that spending time cultivating ourselves again, would remind us of the reasons we had chosen to build life together. We had planned to spend a month in Spain, but the numbers of COVID infections felt daunting. We canceled our

European trip and instead decided to drive to the place that would feel the furthest from us without crossing borders. This is how we ended up in the far southeastern corner of Texas, along the border wall separating us from Juarez.

In the apartment we shared in El Paso, we wrote. Took walks. Drove to exciting nature spots. Talked until we found a way back to each other. But life on the East Coast was calling us, and it was time to turn around and drive back through the vast expanse of Turtle Island to make our way back home.

So, after two weeks spent in El Paso, we packed the house we had called home and drove past large fields protected by barbed wires, all property of the US Army. We said goodbye to a city we had loved, and soaked in the hills and yuccas and rocks and colors. When we drove into the park, the mountains made me weep tears of awe.

The ranger who guided us through the park—a requirement to see the pictographs—told us about the aoudads, and the ways they had adapted to this site, three syenite mountains that look like oversized piles of rocks that had been home to many indigenous lineages before becoming a park. She told us that, as she asked us to reflect on the privilege it was for us all to stand and walk on land that is sacred to people who survived genocide. She asked us to remember that we were on land stolen from people still alive today. She asked that of our group, mostly made up of retired Americans, living year-round in RVs, circling sacred land around Turtle Island. Aside from a young indigenous woman reclaiming the sacred land of her people, we were the youngest in this crowd.

We walked through trails lined with chaparral, ocotillo, and mesquite bushes, surrounded by rocks, as our guide pointed out pictographs from civilizations long gone. Horses, frogs, corn, painted in red pigment in deep corners of the rock formation. Around us, we saw traces of aoudad activity everywhere. Scat mostly. It was then that our guide told us that the aoudad was called the Barbary sheep. She didn't know, but it made me want to meet them. Kin.

* * *

Even if they lived in the American West for multiple generations, aoudads are still considered to be an exotic invasive species on this archeological site, and that means that this herd of aoudads is safe from hunters. Outside of the Hueco Tanks though, they are considered destructive to the Texan landscape and that puts them at risk. An economy of aoudad hunts has developed in the deserts of Texas, and ranchers rent out their land for people to kill them. They capture the aoudads from public lands and relocate them to their private ranches. People are willing to pay a lot of money to shoot a North African goat in the American West.

As our guide talked, I longingly looked at the top of the boulders, silently praying for my long-lost cousins to give me a sign. It would have made sense, I was standing in a sacred space whose beauty reminded me of the meaning of worship. A sign from the universe, reminding me again of ancestral closeness at a time when I was desperate for it.

The aoudads never came to find us, so I looked at pictures and read about them. I learned that as they thrived in the western parts of Texas, displacing the longhorns, their numbers had dwindled in their native Maghreb putting them at risk of extinction. They had become another victim of the explosion of capitalism in the most remote parts of the Maghreb. In that West, jeeps had become too frequent, often driven by people bringing in rifles, eager to kill a sheep. The roads, and new infrastructures progressively destroying their habitat and effectively destroying their chance of survival. The aoudads had switched homes, trading their ancestral West to the West of a new world. Animals failing to adapt to their natural habitat, thriving on foreign soil. Kin.

* * *

Zohara and Eliyahu were part of a large and diverse Jewish community living in the Red City. Until 1948 and the creation of a Zionist State, there were 300,000 Jews living in Morocco, dispersed in the cities' mellahs, the Jewish neighborhoods. Mellah, salt in English, as in the salt marshes of the original neighborhood of Fes, created in 1438 that became the name for all the Jewish neighborhoods around the kingdom. Today, there's a few thousands Jewish people left, mostly in Casablanca, and the various mellahs of the Moroccan kingdom have transformed into other neighborhoods, swallowed by history, and shifting geographies.

When my grandparents were living in the imperial city of Marrakech, there were fifteen thousand others living in the Jewish neighborhood built in the 1560s. You might notice that I say neighborhood and not ghetto, because I don't want you to think that in Morocco, they treated the Jews like they did in Europe. While my European ancestors carry the weight of pogroms, persecution and segregation, life in the Maghreb was different. Before the mellah, the Jews lived amongst the Moors and the Muslims protected by the dhimma, the law of Islam protecting non-muslims' life, religion, and property in exchange for their loyalty to the state. The loyalty was an easy feat, as Judaism believes in dina de-malkhuta dina, the law of the land that is seen as superseding even the laws of Judaism. A well-matched people.

* * *

50 miles away from the imperial city of Marrakech lies the base of the mountains of the High Atlas, the highest range of North Africa. It's a landscape of sparse vegetation and high altitude that has protected its inhabitants from the numerous waves of invasion in the Kingdom. The impenetrable ridge has been the home of many animals who do not survive anywhere else: the bearded vulture, the Barbary leopard, the Atlas day gecko, the aoudad. One of the richest ecosystems in this part of the world. I have never seen the Atlas Mountains.

* * *

In November 1979, on Turtle Island, 116 miles away from the Palo Duro Canyon, a national group of wildlife management experts meets somewhere in the Texas Tech University in Lubbock Texas. They are holding the First Symposium on Ecology and Management of the Barbary sheep, organized by C. David Simpson. Fifty experts are gathered to discuss the ways to address the issues and questions posed by the Barbary sheep that has proliferated on the American continent.

They are discussing what, in ecology, is called an alien species, animals who live outside of their natural home range.

A year later they will publish their proceedings, a small orange booklet, that compiles studies of the herds living in the American West, that has since then become a staple of Barbary sheep studies internationally. Feeding habits, herd compositions and behaviors, histories of migration, the orange booklet paints a picture of this cousin of the goat.

To help us understand the context of this symposium, the editors add to the appendix the Wildlife Society 1975 policy statement on the Introduction of Exotic Species:

> "History reveals that the introduction of exotic flora or fauna into new ecosystems often has been more detrimental than beneficial. Responsible agencies should endeavor to ensure that intentional introduction of exotic species be beneficial and that accidental introductions be prevented. This responsibility relates not only to the protection of human health and livelihood but also to the maintenance of ecological integrity."

Other terms used to describe exotic species: introduced species, adventive species, immigrant species, foreign species, non-indigenous species, non-native species, alien species. Kin.

* * *

In 1999, I walked through the mellah, to visit my great grandparents' grave and take pictures that would be sent back to my mother's parents. My mother had gathered information that led us to follow an old man through the maze of graves of the Miaara cemetery. My mother took pictures with a camera, pictures she'd develop and send to her own parents. The memories are almost gone, yet I remember that after the cemetery we stood in front of my grandfather's childhood home, a riad, that like all riads didn't look like anything from the street. We were a strange group, standing in the middle of the street, my father catching everybody's attention. "Ali Baba, Ali Baba" they would say because that's what people yell in Morocco to Western tourists and my father was one of them. My parents tried to talk to people, tell them that this was the house in which my mother's father was born and the energy in the street shifted drastically.

In that memory, there is a conversation, in which I am being told that there is now a Muslim family living in my grandfather's home, followed by stones being thrown at our carriage as we drive off. Not enough to make sense of a moment.

I learn about the history of the mellah, in my home on Turtle Island, in one of the largest cities of the largest settler-colonial state in human history. Amongst the knick knacks accumulated over the years, I learn about my ancestors' homes in books written in English, by people who have built their careers telling the stories of people who are not theirs. I spend a lot of time in my home thinking about ancestors and ancestral lands. Like everybody in my lineage I am haunted by the dead. I am haunted by a need to make sense of my own place in the world from the fragmented remains left by the forced movement of my elders.

When I think about home and the mellah of my ancestors, I conveniently edit the generation that colonized Palestine. I edit it, because, in this story, I want to place myself on a land that was ours; I want to place myself as part of a lineage of belonging. I edit it because, when I think about home, I do sometimes think about the desert I was born in, but that's a complicated story that me and my body need to reckon with in other settings. When I think about home, I don't want you to think that I believe Palestine to be my home, I need you to know that Palestine should be free from the river to the sea without me in it. I want you to know that all our freedoms depend on it, because there isn't a home for anybody without a free Palestine.

* * *

In 2008, I spent my spring on Turtle Island's former Barbary Coast, currently known as San Francisco. For a few months, I slept on a Laz-E-Boy chair set in the middle of a failing bookstore. At night, I would go to noise and punk shows and come back to the empty store, undress in the dark and sleep in the chair that anybody could see from the street if they paid enough attention.

The owner of the bookstore, Jack, surrounded himself with young immigrants over whom he could rule. In his kingdom, we were all paid under the table and the money was meant to buy our company. I had met Jack the year before, on my first trip to the city, on my first real trip to the United States. That night, I was killing time waiting for my movie at the Roxie, and I lingered in the store. "You're not buying anything," he finally asked, and I explained in my still-thickly-accented English that my suitcases were already full of books, that I was going home the next day. We talked about France and my degrees in publishing, we talked about literature and eventually Jack offered me to come back the following year to live in his store and sell books. I took the chance.

He was my ticket out of France. I was twenty-three and ready to leave my family. I had graduated from an applied art school and ended a relationship; there was nothing tying me to Paris anymore and his offer made it sound like an adventure. So I spent half a year working two jobs and sharing a bed with a friend to save on rent, and when I had saved enough money I flew back to the city. A few months in the center of the Mission, talking about books and exploring this new city. He wanted a friend; I wanted a place to be. It, of course, fell apart quickly.

Jack was obsessed with two things: Charles Bukowski and his ex-wife, a Tunisian woman who had divorced him and worked in the bakery across the street. They had met in her native Maghreb, where he was a tourist and she saw her chance for a new world. After living in her new habitat for some time, she realized that she had to leave him. He couldn't understand that choice and would observe her every move from the window of the store.

I should have seen these two obsessions for the red flags they were but I was desperate. I endured the endless monologues and rants of a lonely man, because my new environment suited me more than my old one.

A few months after I started living in the bookstore, Jack came in at 6am, while I was still asleep, and I realized I had to leave. So, I did what any twenty-three year-old would do: I made him fire me. On days I was alone in the store, I would sneak into the room hidden behind the bookshelf where he hid the expensive books and pick a few to give to friends. I knew Jack would notice, I knew he would have to let me go for betraying his trust.

* * *

The Barbary sheep is endemic to the Atlas Mountains that surround the imperial city of Marrakech. As in, the Barbary sheep has been part of this landscape for millennia, the species' survival intertwined with the shifts of the impenetrable mountains of the Kingdom. A gifted rock-dweller, it can survive in rugged environments deemed inhospitable by most, surviving on little water and sparse vegetation.

The Amazigh people gave it the name aoudad. Amazigh, also known as Berber, as in the indigenous people to the land, meaning the Free men, the majority of people living in the Atlas Mountains, fiercely defending a nomadic way of life threatened by global modernity. Once living in the isolation gifted by altitude, the Amazigh communities have seen their lives change with roads, cars, and accrued tourism.

They say that Safta Zohara's maiden name is Amazigh, that it translates in English to rock. Our people, people of the stones. I wonder when my grandmother's people walked down from their mountain to live in the city that would raise her. I wonder how our people revered the aoudad in this landscape that they had both claimed as home.

Nowadays, there are only 800 to 2000 aoudads remaining in the Kingdom of Morocco, hidden in the mountains, away from the human eye. In Texas, their numbers are estimated to be 5,000 to 10,000. A vulnerable population.

* * *

My body is made out of bones and muscles and mucus, but it is also made out of water, and memories and particles and stardust and magic. Every plant that my ancestors ingested continues to live in my body and every one of their fears became embedded in my DNA. Their experience of their environment shaped the body that I live in today. I wonder if the aoudads of Texas and I have been witnessed by the same landscapes in our ancestral lands. I want to believe that we carry, in our bodies and bones and blood, the particles of the leaves and flowers that saw our lineages past. Kin.

* * *

During my stay in the Chihuahan desert, understanding myself connected to a piece of home, I scheduled a session with an intuitive Jewish healer, who channels the messages of ancestors as a way of healing trauma of our lineage. Over the phone, she introduced me to you, the ancestor I needed to know existed. Hidden in the line of the past, you had been looking over me since the day I was born. You, who chose to live in exile, in the desert of the Maghreb, away from the community that raised you. Kin.

On that day, I learned that the desperation I carry, the immense loneliness that feels impossible to satiate has been yours all along. I learned that the darkness I hold within myself, just like the plants and the landscape is that of my lineage. It's yours, not mine.

This story doesn't start or end with me. We both made the decision to leave home to find ourselves, like Safta Zohara and Saba Eliyahu after you and before me. We all decided to find our identities in lands that weren't ours, even if it meant severing our holy lineage. Even if it meant taking land from its righteous owner and participating in threads of destruction. And in this lineage, I might be the only one to move back into the desert, out of joy rather than necessity.

As you, my beloved ancestor, drowned in the loneliness of your desert life, and Safta Zohara and Saba Eliyahu rooted themselves in a genocidal state, I miraculously held on to hope and found love and care. And on that day, through the lips of a stranger, you told me that watching me root myself into community healed the wounds of our lineage.

* * *

That spring of 2008, after the Laz-E-boy in the Mission District, I moved on to a sublet in a house filled with rainbows and music and crystals in Berkeley. It was the room of a queer I had met while selling books; their mother had died unexpectedly, and they were rushing down South to be with family. Their roommates and I had met before, and we were all part of an extended community I was just getting to know.

There's a cliché about queer and punk communities saving us, about the ways we can hold on to each other and trust that there will be a joy impossible to attain in our bloodlines, and it isn't one that I want to use here even though it did. I want to talk about the joy of reinvention amongst new people. It was easier for me to become myself amongst strangers than it was in a place of expectations. It was easier to hold on to the hope of transformation on foreign soil, than to adapt —again—within my communities of origin.

In the house on Prince Street, I found myself rooting my body into new relationships. I found myself taking on the southern drawl of my roommate and incorporating California slang to my mismatched English. Where my family called me selfish, in California I was thoughtful. Without the shadows cast by those who tried to mold me, I could expand and be witnessed. I noticed my body opening to the possibility of this new person I could become.

I haven't talked to any of my California people in years, but I still see us as intertwined in forever kinship. Our relationship today is punctuated with hearts created by double taps on pictures that document decades passing, but for a short while, they were my home. They made me understand what it meant to be given the space to exist. They taught me that sometimes, in the space of foreignness, we can discover our most authentic selves. Kin.

* * *

In the fall of 2021, in my crumbling home in one of the largest cities of the largest settler-colonial state in human history, I question my choice to live in a country I have come to despise. I feel deeply alienated by the laws of this land. I dream of running away to the Atlas Mountains of my ancestors because I realize I have failed to follow the rules of the land, I have failed to adapt to my new environment.

I have lived on Occupied Lenape land for eight years now, and I spend my days on the phone with people who have been tortured inside prisons, and people who are expecting to be tortured inside prisons. I listen, and I talk, and I advocate. Once a week, or once a month, I iron my blazer and place my badge in my pocket and wear the boots that make me feel taller and I go inside courtrooms, to tell judges all the ways we can avoid prisons. I sign letters of support and talk to probation officers. I withhold and keep secrets, so many secrets. My whole life has prepared me for this task, but these days, I can feel myself triggered when I enter a courtroom, because of all that I have seen in them. I can feel my body rejecting the life I have built. I've just lost a longtime relationship with someone I considered family. I am grieving and I want to blame geography for my grief. *If I were home, I wouldn't feel grief anymore.*

* * *

I live 3,900 miles away from my small hometown of Mulhouse, 3,700 miles from Marrakech, 5,800 miles from the desert where I was born. Aoudads live over 5,000 miles away from home. They thrive in a desert where very few do, by grazing lichens, bushes, and moss from which they gather their water. They roam the Southwest Mountains in nomadic herds. In the literature I read about the aoudads, they are described as colonizers of their environment. Kin.

I feel grief for the aoudads who were displaced from their former land, and who are now hunted in the deserts they have adapted to. I feel grief for them because they are surviving. Isn't that what mountain goats are supposed to do in the desert?

I sit with the contradictions of this world, where nothing feels right anymore. I struggle to find meaning inside the unfolding apocalypse. I turn to the dead for answers.

* * *

A week ago, my estranged mother sends me a string of emails to let me know they're selling my childhood home. I left that home for the last time a decade ago, and with it my relationship with the people who hurt me the most. The emails are in my trash folder, where all her emails get filtered. There's been a lot of emails since I've told her our relationship is over. There's been an incessant flow of unprompted boundary breaches over the years. My mother knows how to make me feel hunted. She knows how to make me feel like no matter how far I go, I cannot escape the environment that raised me.

In her emails, she sends me pictures of pictures that made her sentimental for our relationship. She only sends me pictures where she is happy. She only sends me pictures that mean something to her, not to me. I've always been an accessory to her feelings. In the email is a picture of our 1999 trip to Marrakech. My mother, my father, and I are standing in front of an arch in the medina of Marrakech. I am fourteen years old, my hair is cropped short, and I am wearing bell bottom jeans, platform shoes and a military bag decorated with small paintings made with glow-in-the-dark paint. Just like all the other pictures my mother sends me, I don't recall the photograph ever being taken.

Over the years, her emails have sent me in spirals of shame and rage and grief. She usually writes them as if an invisible audience could read them too, peppering them with niceties, as if we had only forgotten to call each other lately. Her reality is a fiction that she is trying to force me to accept, one in which my silence is unreasonable, unwarranted.

After each email, I will cry, and process and process some more. Each email feels like a pointed reminder that no matter what I do, I will never heal from this. This time around, as I open each picture that she sends, I notice myself moving quicker through the crisis. She cannot touch me anymore; my mother has lost her power over me. I notice myself appreciating the pictures, noting details of my outfit, paying attention to my crooked childhood teeth. I download the pictures and drag the message to the trash again.

After I close my computer, I sit with the news. They are selling our home. I will never see my childhood room again; I will never have access to the books and records and trinkets I left behind. A signed Bukowski novel given by Jack, my favorite books, a notebook. I was never going to be able to do that anyway, but the certainty hits my solar plexus with force. I guess this is what my mother wanted me to feel, because grief is the only way she will ever have access to me again.

A few days later, as I continue to think about this email, I end up grateful for the reminder of her cruelty because it cuts through the nostalgia that sometimes engulfs me. In times when the guilt of leaving, the guilt of starting over becomes unbearable, I think about the emails that discard my own feelings. The reasons why I had to rebuild myself elsewhere. And there is no shortage of nostalgia or guilt; I don't think you ever move on from leaving a life behind. I don't think your body ever adjusts, and mine still wants to hop on a plane, knock on my mother's door and let her caress my hair while crushing my soul until I am so small I disappear. I don't think you change languages and foods and continents without ever feeling like you made a mistake. A wish to rewind and try another path.

Nostalgia is a funny feeling. It is the memory of something that wasn't quite that, and that will never be again. I remember my homelands in ways that they might have been, but never will be again. My mother remembers me differently than I ever was; I never came out to her because it never felt safe. I remember her as whoever she was ten years ago and every single detail I glean from her unhinged, desperate attempts at touching me since then. She probably learns about who I am through her Internet searches, trying to find remnants of the child I used to be, rejecting every bit that doesn't match her memory of me.

And I do that too, when I let myself linger in the memory of the mellah for too long, when I imagine myself, an aoudad climbing Jbel Toubkal, and when I try to rebuild memories from books and Internet searches. When I idealize a life that others left, a life rendered impossible in this version of the world. I am nostalgic for a life that was never mine, in a desert that only lives in my body because of the nostalgia of others. Kin.

Thinking about Na3na3

WE HAVE BEEN EXPERIENCING INTENSE HEAT WAVES IN Philadelphia, unrelenting swelter that doesn't evaporate even in the darkest hours of the night. Over the years, I have gotten used to the sticky and humid summers, but lately it has felt oppressing. When the heat permeates the early hours of the day, I am transported to mornings in my grandparent's front yard, a tiled outdoor space with a table covered in a thick plastic tablecloth, lightly dusted with sand. There used to be lemon trees along the edges, and then just tiles.

My grandparents lived in B'ir al-Sab, currently known as Beer-Sheva within the Zionist State. A small first floor of a house, a yard on top of a sandy hill wrapped by an iron-wrought gate, in front of the city hall. I fear the sandy hill doesn't exist anymore, swallowed by construction. My grandparents are long gone.

But back then I spent part of my summers there, with my mother and my siblings. We'd sleep in the Heder Aravi, their Arab room. An assortment of large rugs and paintings of the desert separated from the rest of the house with a curtain of wooden beads, mementos of a life left in the old country. In the Heder Aravi, the furniture was set up so that an imaginary tea ceremony could happen at a moment's notice; the center of the room left unused for a fictional group to sit cross-legged and share warm beverages. Nobody used the room for tea drinking. Aside from the occasional guest, the room also hosted an extra fridge, holding large bottles of soda and baskets of stone fruits.

In the mornings we would drink coffee, made the Turkish way, and Nes, or na3na3 tea, the Moroccan way, in those translucent glass mugs with a handle that are omnipresent in Occupied Palestine. Early, before the desert sun burnt everything, before the shade would disappear and be replaced by blinding light. A tea bag, fresh mint leaves, a healthy dose of sugar. The cooling properties of a plant known for growing rapaciously, preparing us for the ruthless heat of the desert. We would sit in the coolness of the early morning, around the table covered in a thick plastic tablecloth, lightly dusted with sand.

When I was younger, my grandmother would have baked us dry cookies to dip into our drink. Some covered in sesame, some plain. A hint of orange blossom, maybe. As she grew older, she would outsource that task and buy them from a neighbor. A couple of biscuits, mint leaves, floating in glass cups. Mint leaves in a mug at home, as an act of care for my mother back in Mulhouse.

They say that holding a cup of hot beverage is akin to a hug to the nervous system. I think about the generations of ancestors, who before me and my mother and my grandmother brewed herbs in hot water. I think about the way I already existed in my grandmother's body when she herself made tea, pregnant with my mother, and the way she was present in her grandmother's body. Seeds witnessing our lineage's tradition. A practice of pouring water over the plants available to us, to let them remind us that we are loved along our whole line.

Tea means something in the Moroccan lineage of my grandparents. In Arab societies, tea means generosity and care and hospitality. Tea means that I want your company enough that I will boil the water and wait for the beverage to be ready. In tea, my people understand themselves as people of connections and relationships.

Nowadays, when I make my morning tea that changes with the seasons I am doing something that my ancestors did for centuries before me: crush a plant and pour boiling water on it. Often it is mint, because mint is the plant closest to my heart. I have never lived without her, and she has seen my people shift across the globe, chasing a freedom that would always elude them. Mint has seen worlds change and human civilizations rise and fall and continues to grow. Mint won't turn into tea unless I wait for it to steep.

We call it Maghrebi tea, Tuareg tea, Moroccan tea, or Moroccan whisky, the mix of mint and tea and sugar that is drunk throughout the day to support the body in the desert. Yet, I often think about the ways the tea that we understand as quintessentially Moroccan is global, a result of capitalism and colonialism. How Moroccan mint tea is a mix of mint and gunpowder green tea, Chinese tea brought in by the British as they pillaged the African continent. Sugar brought in by boats to the port of Essaouira, connected to the commerce of human bodies. In mint tea, I think about the ways our traditions and ways of understanding ourselves always start somewhere, and that more often than not, the ways we define ourselves are closer to us than we think.

Mint is maybe the most beloved medicinal plant, probably because of her gentleness coupled with her ability to grow and adapt in most environments. Mint is a genus (*Mentha* in its botanical name) encompassing 42 species and a variety of hybrids and subspecies, but usually when we talk about mint, we might be describing peppermint or spearmint. Plants of the *Mentha* genus all have in common a square stem and opposite leaves, and the magical ability to release smell when touched. The Ancient Greek would rub the plant on their arms to get stronger; today we use mint for digestive issues, to relieve the body from nausea, for the pleasure of taste.

Mint, especially commercial mint, is not considered native to North America; colonizers of the land brought her in in the vessels of the manifest destiny. With the pillages of the natural world was born pharmaceutical commerce and the industrial use of the mint flavor: in toothpaste and candy and cigarettes. But Morocco is still the number one producer of mint in the world, growing 90% of the world's spearmint and peppermint.

In the summer of 1999, in the imperial city of Marrakech, tour guides handed us bouquets of mint as we walked around the tanneries. It was incredibly hot that day, like every day in the city, and I was wearing more clothes than I wanted because of the constant harassment in the streets. We walked past the piles of animal skin and the humongous vats of quicklime. An overpowering smell of death surrounded us, as the guide reminded us to hold the mint under our nose. My mother gagged and gagged as we laughed, giving her some of ours to mitigate the sensory overload she was experiencing.

This year, I've been growing Moroccan mint (na3na3—*Mentha longifolia*) which is different from your usual spearmint, stronger, more floral, a lighter green, softer leaves. I can't find the na3na3 I want in the stores in the US; I often end up with a bag of American spearmint, so different from the taste of my childhood so I found seeds to grow under the blue and pink grow lights I keep in my kitchen during Philadelphia winters.

The seeds have grown into plant and now, in my garden, I have a pot full of na3na3. I feel a little shy around her, the feeling of two separate worlds colliding. I am meeting my old self in the pot of my new life. I admire her leaves, I touch her gently, I get to know her again. She's lighter in color than the other mints I grow, and her smell touches my spine and opens my chest in a way that no other plant can.

She brings me back to smaller versions of me, the obedient child who turned on the kettle and got the mug and put the herb in the mug and waited before walking from the kitchen to the bedroom, to give my mother what she requested. She brings me back to the delicate care of an elder boiling the water and putting the leaves and the tea and the sugar and the spoon and walking from the kitchen through the living room and the dining corner, opening the door and bringing me a mug as I sit in the front yard. She reminds me that as imperfectly as I was loved, I was loved, and that that love was an ancestral one, one that passed on from my mother to her mother to her mother. That the plant that was crushed and offered to me in hot water, that mint, was herself a witness of my own people, that she had experienced the pain and the joy and the destruction that come with human life.

I feel overwhelmed by shyness around this plant that I am growing for the first time, in my home garden, surrounded by plants that I have known for many seasons. In other parts of the garden, I see myself as adventurous, opinionated, daring; around the na3na3 I tinker, and caress, offering her the reverence I was taught to bestow to elders. It's the classic feeling connected to diaspora: "Am I enough to claim this part of my lineage?" An incessant hum, the embarrassment of not speaking the language of my ancestors, of having severed ties with my roots —the ultimate desecration in the tradition of my people.

So instead of tending to the roots of my people, I tend to the plants in my backyard, including my na3na3 plant. She's happy in my backyard, growing in a large pot that fills up more with each growing season, as she is a perennial. Meaning she will come back to me every year, growing deeper roots and stronger connection to the soil she lives in.

There's a different relationship that happens with plants when you grow them. You learn their rhythm, their favorite temperature. The insects who like to nibble on their leaves. You get to pay attention to their growth, how many more shoots are growing this year. The labor that is required to keep them alive. As a gardener, you can't take your love for granted. You can't believe that just having the best of intentions yields the best results: you learn the plant, what she wants and you adapt. How much happier she is moved to this corner. How she reacts after the heavy rains. When she goes to sleep for the season and when she comes back.

Mint doesn't usually get cultivated from seeds, as her roots system quickly multiplies, creating offshoots that can live feet away from their mother plant. To grow mint, gardeners will slice a part of the plant and move it to another corner and wait a season. The cut mint limb will become whole if given the time. Gardeners will warn you, wherever you put mint she will overtake, growing far past the boundaries of the life you had set up for her. She will burst out of beds, finding new crevices to build new life. Seasoned gardeners will tell you: plant your mint in a pot or allow her to reign.

Mint, the ubiquitous plant often overlooked for nicer, shinier plants, builds her kingdom one root at a time until she has taken over space that wasn't meant for her, adapting to the conditions in front of her. It's hard to kill a mint plant, she doesn't need much support; a plant that favors neglect. She loves moisture and sun, but will survive droughts if needed. One of the hardier plants I know, she will die in the winter and come back voraciously in the spring. Sometimes, when the winters are mild she'll just stay alive, less fragrant, less majestic but still alive.

Every morning, I spend a few minutes in the garden, saying hello to each one of my plants: hops, rue, yarrow, lemon balm and wood betony. Mountain mint and tulsi. Hawthorn and sage. Dyer's chamomile and anise hyssop. The fennel and the echinacea. Motherwort and elder trees. There's a floral cornucopia in the backyard, and each plant means something else to me. A story, an anecdote, a moment in time where I needed to cultivate that relationship to find my center again.

I grow other mints in my backyard: mountain mint and spearmint. Pennyroyal too. But the na3na3, oh the na3na3, she will always be my favorite. Simple green leaves growing in a pot over a system of roots capable of taking over worlds. My favorite smell. Every once in a while, I'll pick a few leaves to chew on and to make a fresh pot of tea with. And the taste brings me back to those mornings in the hot sun, at the table with the thick tablecloth. In those moments I imagine myself as the adult guiding a child towards the rituals of mornings.

Fruits of the Desert

A DECADE AGO, ON MY WAY TO THE FOOD CO-OP IN ANN Arbor, I played the game I have played my whole life where a stranger asks me what I am, and I let them guess my ethnicity. Depending on the country I'm in and the way I am dressed, people assume that I'm Colombian, Punjabi, Syrian, Turkish. I'm believed to be *something*, so they guess. Can they see the edges of Morocco in the shape of my eyes? Can they feel like I am the product of many colonizations? How could they guess that I am a Jewish Arab, born a settler to Palestine?

This man, leaning against the front door of the store I was trying to enter, was somewhat better than most. He called me a Sabra, a term I had never used to describe myself, yet fitting for the circumstances of my birth.

Sabra. A term invented by the Zionist State to describe Jewish people born in Occupied Palestine. Sabra, the Hebrew word for my favorite fruit. Sabra. A move to create a national(ist) identity from scratch, a way of uniting vastly different diasporic identities into one rooted in a plant abundant in the deserts of Palestine.

In English, Sabra is the prickly pear—the fruit of a cactus, a marvel really that such sweetness can grow in the desert. Out of the thorns of one of nature's most resilient plants, oblong fruits grow in a myriad of warm colors: red, yellow, orange, pink. Little color-packed miracles that defy our understanding of ecology. Each fruit covered in thorns so thin, they're almost invisible to the human eye.

Calling Israelis Sabra is supposed to be a clever metaphor: Jews born within the Zionist State have tough exteriors and sweet insides, just like the cactus fruit. It is a thin thread to connect a nation around, but what histories of colonialism have shown us is that it's enough to create new shared identities.

Calling Israelis Sabra is also another humiliation inflicted to the people indigenous to the land, who themselves have used the prickly pear as a symbol of belonging for generations before their dispossession and who are now left to use it as a symbol of their resistance and sustained existence in the face of genocide.

In Palestine, they say saber as-sabbar, "the patience of the cactus," to describe the resilience of the people living on a land not always kind. The people indigenous to Palestine saw their lives reflected in the thorny fruit of the cactus: like them it was resilient in duress, like them it thrived in a somewhat harsh environment, like them the plant extended generosity by using its resources towards creating a sweet fruit during the hottest month of July. In Palestine, the fruit of the cactus would be eaten communally, cut in slices by the men and shared with all.

Because before there was a Zionist State there was land farmed by families who would use the prickly pear as fences between their fields, the thorns of the cactus creating a natural barrier.

Before there was a Zionist State, the fellahins grew wheat and barley and olive trees and grapes and figs. They developed farming techniques that required little to no irrigation. A necessity on a land that lacked water.

Before there was a Zionist State there was an Ottoman Empire and a British Mandate; before there was a Zionist State some of the land belonged to absentee landlords, a lot more of it was duly owned by the families tending the land. Before there was a Zionist State, belonging to the land didn't always mean deeds and records and ownership but it sometimes did. In Palestine, those who understood the land, those who were of the land were its righteous owners. As a collective, a community.

418 Palestinian villages were destroyed to make way for the Zionist State. I almost typed each village name so that we could collectively remember them. I wanted to write their names but I worried you wouldn't read them. I worried that their names alone wouldn't convey the scale of the annihilation. I worried that you would think I did it as a performance and not as a prayer for their return. 418 communities, with people, houses, stores, and fields, razed to make way for a new reality that wanted them erased. 418 communities razed also meaning death, expulsions, dispossession, and a life of survival in the refugee camps in Jordan and Syria and Lebanon. In each one of the villages, I imagine a circle, and a man holding a knife and an oblong fruit, generously sharing sweetness with his neighbors.

Sabra. The Zionist State spread the term before 1948, to help propagate the idea of Israel being built by farmers, to make sense of the privately owned cooperatives and the collectively owned kibbutzim. *Through their hard work European Zionists transformed the empty land of Palestine into a green utopia.* A lie that many, including my own people, still believe.

* * *

In 1901, three years before his death, Theodore Hertzl led the Fifth Zionist Congress at the Stadt Casino, in Basel Switzerland, less than 24 miles from my home of Mulhouse. It's on that day that the Jewish National Fund was created, for the purpose of buying Palestinian land towards a Zionist goal. In Hebrew, we know it as the Keren Kayemet, a biblical reference of the good deeds accomplished in buying land and planting trees that will result in bounty to be enjoyed in another life, after the Messiah's return. All land bought by the Keren Kayemet LeIsrael is to be "the property of Jewish people for perpetuity," as if land could be owned and claimed instead of revered. All over the world, Jewish families like mine put their change in blue boxes for that specific cause of collectively buying property for Jewish people for perpetuity. All over the world, Jewish families like mine are being tricked into believing in the idea that the fund created beauty on empty Palestinian land by planting trees and creating green landscapes in a place where nothing grew. Today, Keren Kayemet owns up to 13% of what used to be Palestine. Most of the forests they plant grow on the ruins of 418 destroyed Palestinian villages.

Settler-colonialism feeds on ideals of "back to the land" models, of occupation of native crops. It takes what's around it, appropriates it, destroys it. But if the colonizers believe that they are meant to be on this land, they can come together, find common ground. This idea of a nation cemented the hierarchy of Israeli society.

* * *

In the summer of 2002, Palestinian filmmaker Michel Khleifi and Israeli filmmaker Eyal Sivan, set off to document life along the imaginary line of the proposed partition of Palestine in 1947. It became a movie they called *Route 181*. Watching it, I feared that accents, racialized assumptions, and definitions of Jewishness and Arabness would be lost in translation to most. I watched it in snippets because the brutality of the Zionist society destroyed my nervous system. I was transported to my time being detained at the airport for refusing to carry an Israeli passport and to my time pleading with a ranked officer in a mix of English and German to note in the thick file he had in front of him that I didn't need to serve in the Zionist occupation forces. I was reminded of the times being stopped at the border because, even if I didn't need to serve anymore, I was a disgrace to my country of birth for not enrolling. I watched the documentary in beds and couches, taking long breaks to drink water and numb myself.

In the movie, an older woman tells the story of her family's dispossession. She was thirteen during the Nakba and she fled her village of Al-Shajara barely avoiding death as it became one of the 418 villages erased from maps. She relocated to Tur'an, 3 miles away, where she is filmed.

She tells the camera, "I would so love to see Al-Shajara. A prickly pear tree. An olive tree. The shade of a low wall. I'm dying to smell its scent. The refugees in Syria asked me for a fistful of its earth so they can smell its scent. My precious homeland."

* * *

In French, we call the prickly pear *Figue de Barbarie*, or Barbary Coast fig, an old-timey term to describe the portion of the African Coast between Morocco and Libya, where my ancestors thrived. That's where the French encountered the fruit for the first time, in their own destructive expeditions towards land they would steal a century later. But again, the prickly pear isn't native to the Barbary Coast, or the Middle East for that matter. It finds its roots in the Americas, moved around to Spain after the 15th century before being introduced to the Maghreb. They say that in his genocidal travels, Columbus traveled with prickly pears, feeding his people the nopal to fend off scurvy. My people do not eat the cactus, they only savor its fruits.

In Morocco they call it elhendi, Indian fig, and the massive quantities of prickly pears cultivated in the country are moved to French supermarkets by global supply chains. Trucks crossing the country and the Gibraltar strait. Trucks moving through borders inaccessible to humans in need of safety.

* * *

As a child, I adored sabras—the intricate ways to open them without getting pricked by it, the different flavors depending on the color of the pear. I even enjoyed the thrill of the invisible thorns that covered my hands more times than I would like to admit.

My mother would buy them at the market and open them for me, expertly peeling the prickly skin away from the delicious flesh. I adored their sweetness and the slight variations of flavor depending on the different colors. She would slice them and place them on a plate, juices pooling and tinting the ceramic. I don't remember any of my siblings eating sabra with us; it was our own little delight, a gift. I don't remember using the French word to describe them; one of those intimate moments with my mother spoken in our shared native language. Now I wonder if the only reason I was introduced to that fruit was because of my mother's deep belief in the State of Israel. If the fruit was a memory of her own time spent in the kibbutz during her military service.

Or if it was part of my grandparents foodways, if they had grown up getting prickly pears in the markets of Marrakech. If they, too, had experienced the juices tinting their faces shades of orange and purple. If they had reveled in the fruit of their childhood being wildly abundant on this new land they settled and decided to continue the legacy by feeding it to their children. Did my grandparents also introduce their children to this fruit that required careful peeling? Did they feed my mother pieces of purple and orange?

* * *

In early September 2021, Mahmoud Al-Ardah and five other men escaped the Zionist prison of Gilboa, where they were all sentenced to live because of their resistance to the occupation of their ancestral land. They dug a tunnel with spoons, patiently dreaming about freedom on the other side. They didn't communicate with anybody on the outside for fear of repercussions, they just dug.

In an article published after the escape, Al-Ardah describes the amazing taste of the cactus fruit, after twenty-two years of incarceration. A cartoon shows him hugging the cactus tree, the symbol of his people and their history. The cartoon shows him being embraced by the cactus tree in return. When I read the news of the Gilboa escapes I cried. It was on a day where I felt despair and that miraculous story reminded me of the ways we find freedom. Slowly, with determination.

When I read about Mahmoud Al-Ardah, I cried again. Because prison in all its cruelty reproduces the abomination of colonialism by taking land away, by disconnecting us from plants and ecosystems and ancestral practices. The purpose of prison is to take us so far away from land and community and relationship that we forget that we belong to each other, and to the seeds, the birds, the sun, the sky.

I understand the need to be embraced by a plant to feel alive. I understand that in freedom we remember our allegiances, our kinships. I understand what it means to reclaim yourself through your connection with the land.

I wonder what Mahmoud Al-Ardah's memories of the prickly pear are? Does he have favorite colors of it? Did he pick them directly from the cactus? Did he wear plastic bags around his hands to avoid being pricked? Or did he remember an elder cutting the fruit for him, patiently, expertly, and feeding him the gift of the desert? Did he remember that in the saber, the prickly pear, there was community, and laughter, and generosity and ritual? Or did it remind him of everything that was taken away from him by the people who raised me?

Plante Persistante

ON A SPRING DAY OF THE EARLY PANDEMIC, I LOSE MY FA-
vorite ring in my Philadelphia home. I lose it inside my
house, between meetings, after wearing it on a Zoom call,
and not wearing it the day after. It is somewhere but I don't know
where. I retrace my steps and dig through the various trash cans around
the house. It is my favorite ring, a large wormwood leaf made from silver with a small turquoise stone embedded at the center. I bought this
ring from a beloved jeweler as a magical armor meant to remind me of
my own powers, my own ability to heal. It felt so lucky that they sold
a one-of-a-kind ring of a plant that my friend, herbalist Layla Feghali
would call a plantcestor. I feel defeated; I feel a grief too intense for
losing a ring, an oversized feeling for the loss of an object.

I would be lying to you if I failed to admit that I write this para-
graph in the hopes that it will make the ring magically reappear.

* * *

One of my earliest memories is of being detained in a department store
with my mother. It's a foundational memory, one that I return to often
when trying to understand my relationship to France, my relationship

to my mother, the two fault lines that precipitated my migration, our estrangement, my exile.

Like most stories of my childhood, it is a memory never discussed, that only survives as a faded collection of sensations, furtive images, gaps in the narrative. Delicate muscle memory that rips like paper if examined for too long. Over the years, I have turned it over countless times, in a few minutes' increments, hoping to glean details from the act of rewinding and replaying, hoping to make sense of myself.

My parents had been invited to a party, and to prepare, my mother, holding my hand, walked to the Globe at the center of our town. A large department store, filled with luxury brands, scintillating chandeliers, and dark wooden furniture, a building we usually entered to browse without ever buying anything. But it was a special occasion, and she wanted to look good. She was searching for a shirt on which to layer her jacket and on the second floor she found a beautiful black silk tank top adorned with delicate lace. Back then, in her early thirties, my mother took pride in her appearance, and she wanted to impress the people she would be meeting that night. Of the silk tank top, I remember its shine, and I imagine my mother caressing its softness before deciding on the purchase. An extravagance she allowed herself for a night of joy.

I imagine her folding the tank top gently, letting the silk melt into a smaller shape. I imagine her carrying the small package to the register and unfolding the money she held in her purse. I imagine the small burst of delight in her chest, the simple excitement of the perfect garment.

The next part of the story is dim, a faded image I see of the two of us, still hand in hand, on the escalator taking us back downstairs. I can't see a shopping bag in my mother's hand or the clothes we are wearing, but I remember the smell of the rubber, the grooves of the escalator's steps, the specific light that enveloped us. And I remember the security guard who followed us, a large white man wearing a dark uniform. "Where is your receipt?" he must have asked my mother. And I don't know why there wasn't a bag or a receipt, why the guard decided that he should whisk us away to the hidden office at the side of the store. *This Arab woman must have stolen it.* I'm not sure how old I was, somewhere between four and six, and I know that my mother still spoke little French. I wonder why the cashier on the second floor didn't tell them she had just processed the purchase, or explained why my mother wasn't carrying the tank top in the store's bag. I remember a desk, but my body tightens, my stomach clenches if I try to remember much more. The familiar twisting of my insides, an unspooling. All that remains of that memory is this: after what felt like hours, my mother called my father who called a lawyer, we were released, the guard was fired.

A week later, the manager of the store invited us back in to pick an item of our choosing each, a way of making amends. I had imagined myself leaving the store with the latest doll, a toy too expensive for my parents to purchase. Instead, he walked me towards the stand holding the costume jewelry sold to children, the appropriate value of our humiliation. I looked at the display of plastic painted silver and gold, the rings and bracelets adorned with gems made of cheap glass and picked a necklace I would lose soon afterwards.

* * *

Like my mother before me, I was born in Soroka hospital, a settler of Palestine. Like my mother before me, I was born in the desert, the same desert where my parents' unlikely encounter took place. A desert that birthed us, that we would leave too fast for my mind to remember, yet forever shaping me. A desert my mother, my sibling, our dog Lucille and I would leave six months after my birth, flying to the city of Mulhouse, France to join my father who like many immigrant men, was building us a life to move into. None of us had ever lived in that city, but it was close enough to where my father had grown up to feel like a return of sorts.

* * *

Those first few years were a shock to our systems as the borderlands of France are not known for their hospitality towards foreigners. It wasn't an easy home to build for any of us; adapting to this new life was a cruel reality.

Uprooted, my mother turned to the rituals of our ancestors, making sure to always keep na3na3 (mint) and shiba (tree wormwood) in the fridge. Silent witnesses of her own mother's home that had evolved along our people; she would use them to make tea. A bunch of na3na3 leaves in hot water, a sprig of shiba to add bitterness, often drunk at the end of the day.

* * *

In all my kindergarten school pictures, I am dressed in traditional Jacadi dresses, poofy messes of bows and lace representing the epitome of French elegance to my mother. Along with the piano lessons, the rigorous expectation of perfect grades and the rules about table manners we were forced to follow, the dresses were a way to usher me into an idea of Europeanness that my mother craved for all of us.

In my last kindergarten picture, the dress is white, covered with a pattern of pastel flowers, its Peter pan collar trimmed with pink lace, a dress not made for a clumsy five-year-old with a tendency for spillage.

The day of the picture, my mother came to the school, pulled me out of my classroom armed with a brush and made me change out of my already stained clothes, and I probably complied because I was a silent child, an anxious child. She forced me into uncomfortable tights a few shades too light, the dress and ballerina shoes, before taming my frizzy hair with vigorous brushstrokes and an expertly positioned velvet headband to keep it all in place. I had to look perfect for this memory of my childhood, a perfect French child, a model immigrant.

* * *

In Mulhouse, Wednesdays and Saturdays were farmers market days, and my mother would walk the ten minutes from our apartment to the gathering of stalls to buy our groceries: fruits, vegetables, barely expired yogurts sold at a deep discount. Whatever we needed to sustain us for the week would be found there, cheaply, and abundantly, acquired after haggling, the same way her own father would in the stalls of their desert home.

At the end of her shopping, before returning home, my mother would always stop by the smaller stands run by older Maghrebi men, immigrants of France's former colonies in North Africa, who only sold a few offerings laid out on makeshift tables: na3na3, shiba, louisa, herbs of the old country called by their Arabic names, not their French ones. Those men, who sold my mother small bundles of home, looked like my uncles, like my grandfather, and yet she saw them as strangers, as enemies. Arabs.

* * *

My mother loved her na3na3 and shiba tea. She'd ask us to boil the water and put the leaves, no sugar because of her diabetes. She would demand that we make her tea, because she deserved to wield some power and we were the easiest target.

I never understood why she didn't add the tea bags like her mother would; I didn't understand then the power of four green leaves in hot water on the nervous system. I loved na3na3, her sweet and fruity smell; I hated the acrid bitterness of shiba, which tasted like punishment.

* * *

In my first herbalism class, in early 2019, we introduced ourselves to the circle by telling the group what brought us to deepening our relationship to plants. When it was my turn to speak, I told the room about my need to reconnect with land after spending so many years working in the dehumanizing context of prisons, my need to reclaim a lineage beyond my mother's ideals of whiteness. In the herbal traditions of Arab Jews, I believed I could find healing.

My teachers asked me "What are the plants of your ancestors?" and, before na3na3 even, shiba came to me. I drew an elaborate tea pot, one of those metal ones that are omnipresent in Arab families, a replica of the one my grandparents kept but didn't use. I drew the teapot, I drew the plant and I researched shiba, learning about all her siblings around the world, until I found her. *Artemisia arborescens.* I learned that she is native to Morocco, Algeria, Tunisia, Libya, the Levant, Southern Europe. I learned that she is what botanists call a naturalized alien in France.

And when I tasted shiba in hot water again, I realized that my taste buds had changed since childhood and that the lingering sharpness brought the pleasure of belonging.

* * *

"*Toi et tes copines, ces pétasses.* You and your little friends, little bitches. *J'vous ai vu dans la rue rigoler comme des frehas.* I saw you laughing on the street, vulgar bitches. *T'as pas honte?* You have no shame?

You're not sick of bringing us shame? *T'en as pas marre de nous foutre la honte?* Acting like a racaille. *Tu t'comportes comme une racaille.* A whore. *Une pute,*" my mother yells, her face distorted by rage as my father restrains her.

I had known, going up the stairs of our building, that I was late coming home from school, and had tried calming my nerves by counting the tiles, knowing that there would be severe consequences once I reached our apartment door.

Hand on the railing, I walked slowly, trying to compose myself. My transgression: strolling around town, arm in arm with my friends Khadija and Fatouma, strolling the pedestrian downtown of Mulhouse, laughing, as a thirteen-year-old child, and arriving home an hour after school let out that day. My mother didn't like my friends, continuously trying to have me befriend the white children of doctors, instead of the children whose lives and features looked like mine.

Finally, I arrived on the third floor, and as soon as I opened the door, she lunged at me, blocking the hallway with her body, spit flying out of her mouth as she screamed her insults. I am sure that there were more than insults that day, but my body can't quite bring me back to them.

What I do remember vividly, though, is that the next day, as I entered the schoolyard, so did my mother. She was still furious from the day before, pacing amongst middle schoolers until she found them, screaming at Khadija and Fatouma. "*Et si je vous vois avec ma fille, ça va mal se finir pour vous deux. Vous m'avez bien compris?*" she yelled, as their eyes grew bigger from confusion. As quickly as she entered, she was gone and, again, all I can remember of that moment is my own tears shed in the counselor's office, my body trying to hold on to a dignity that I had just lost.

"And if I ever see you again with my daughter, it won't end well for you. You got me?"

* * *

Shiba is what we call, in French, a *plante persistante*, what we call evergreen in English, meaning that given the right environment, soil and climate, she does not lose leaves with the seasons changing, steadily remaining a shimmering bush of silver, flowering with yellow buds.

She is added to the traditional tea when mint gets sparser in Moroccan winters. She is the bitter counterpart to the sweet and cooling na3na3, a quality that warms and fortifies the weakened winter body. I don't remember drinking shiba tea in my grandmother's house in the desert, but I also don't remember many winter visits. I remember the smell of shiba in the markets of Occupied Palestine, and I'm sure that she grows abundantly there too. Maybe if I had still been living there, if my parents' regular threats of moving us to Jerusalem had materialized, I, too, would have looked forward to the bitter cup warming my body at the end of a long day.

I wonder if my mother did drink that tea at home in the desert, or if her farmer's market purchases were her own way of reclaiming a lineage that felt more and more distant with every winter spent in our cold home at the German and Swiss borders.

* * *

As I reconnected with shiba, limited by what plants were available to me on this continent, I turned to her cousin wormwood and sat with a bush at the botanical garden by my house, in Southwest Philadelphia.

I let my fingers caress her silver leaves, soft like the skin of a nurturing parent. Each stroke releasing her pungent smell, woody and floral, each stroke bringing back memories of my mother. In that moment of reunion with a plant of my people, I heard a soft bristling, a voice saying, "Ya benti. I got this, I got this, let it go."

* * *

"Oriental [sic] people usually typify sorrow, cruelty, and calamity of any kind by plants of a poisonous nature. Since the Hebrews considered all bitter-tasting plants to be poisonous, the 'root of wormwood' and the 'wormwood and the gall' would offer to them a most emphatic and unmistakable metaphor."

On Passover night, it is tradition to dip bitter herbs into salted water, to remember the plight of our people, enslaved in the kingdom of Egypt. A remembrance of grief as a power, of grief as a dedication to survival.

* * *

In the kingdom of Caria, in what is currently known as Anatolia, ruler Mausolus dies, survived by his wife and sister Artemisia Caria II. To commemorate his life, she commissions the Mausoleum of Halicarnassus in present-day Bodrum, a large building of marble and columns, filled with statues of the finest quality. The Mausoleum of Halicarnassus becomes known as one of the Seven Wonders of the World along with the Temple of Artemis, the Hanging Gardens of Babylon and the Colossus of Rhodes.

But even a Wonder of the World was not a fitting resting place for the man who had defined her life. Legend has it that Artemisia Caria II chose to instead ingest his ashes, mixing small mounds of charred bones and tissues with her daily drink, a ritual she would perform until her own death two years later.

Artemisia Caria II was known to be a naval strategist, the ruler of a kingdom, and believed to be a skilled herbalist, but history forever remembers her as a woman disfigured by grief, choosing to live her days in the bitterness of becoming her husband's tomb.

In botany, Artemisia Caria II is known for giving her name to a genus of diverse plants found on most continents, including *Artemisia absinthium* and her cousin *Artemisia Arborescens*, respectively known to me as wormwood and shiba.

* * *

Our guts contain 500 million neurons, connected to our brain: the gut-brain axis, connecting our nervous system to the inside of our bellies. My herbalist friend tells me that to heal from the trauma of my childhood, I need to ingest more bitter herbs. She tells me that on top of all the adaptogens that will rebuild my frayed nervous system, bitter herbs will help my body reconnect with itself. Shiba can help me repair the damages inflicted by my caretakers.

* * *

In November 2019, I came back to France, this time because I missed Paris so much, I thought I would explode. By then, I had done enough healing that I was ready to go back to my favorite city without fearing the possibility of running into a family member. It had been seven years since I last went home, since I last entered our apartment in Mulhouse, since I had my last fight with my mother.

"Je n'en ai rien à foutre. C'est ton argent, et alors? J't'ai dit que j'avais une réduction? Toi et ton père, vous pensez qu'vous êtes au-dessus de nous. Appelle le salon, dis-leur de te donner ta réduc'. Pourquoi tu ne m'écoutes pas, hein ? Pourquoi?

"Maman, c'est mon argent, j'vois pas en quoi ça te regarde si j'ai eu une réduc' ou pas."

"Ha c'est ça hein, ton argent, ton argent. T'es chez moi, têtue comme une putain de mule. Tu veux que je me tue? C'est ça? Tu veux tuer ta mère?"

The last time I had seen my mother, she had forced me to get my body waxed clean because she still could not understand why I preferred my legs, armpits and face covered in dark hair. She thought it made me look dirty, that my hair made me look like what she had tried to deny her whole life. I had been visiting for two weeks that summer and finally decided to comply to escape another fight, but as I left the salon, forgot to ask the person checking me out for a discount that my mother thought I was owed.

Her rage had gone on for days, escalating as I refused to call the salon back, arguing that I was paying with my own money and felt no need to pay less. We sat at a standstill, she yelled, telling me that in my stubbornness I was killing her. That she would kill herself if I didn't call the woman back and I complied, one last time.

* * *

In Paris, so many years later, I still noticed the tightening in metro stations, the anxious loop of possible encounters, but their intensity was manageable now. It was the first time I took Johnny, my partner, through the city that saw me turn twenty and twenty-five, and it was the first time I was there without a blood family to visit.

I wanted to find the shiba of my childhood to bring to my new home and I searched for her in the North African stores of Barbès and la Goutte d'Or. I saw her fresh in the meat markets of the Boulevard de Barbès, and in that small bakery next to the Guerrisol thrift store, but I needed her dry to fly back to what was home now. I surrendered and purchased a small bag at an overpriced apothecary by the Palais-Royal, surrounded by English-speaking tourists. Not quite the same, in my defeat, I was reminded of the distance that now existed between me and the streets of this place I still considered home, so many years later.

What is meant for me will find me if I put my attention to it. I looked and looked, and she was nowhere I wanted to find her, in this big city that had raised me more thoroughly than my mother ever did.

And then I found her. I found shiba in a place so obvious that I didn't even consider it a possibility. We met again at the Jardin des Plantes, the former royal gardens filled with conquered plants of France's past, as I walked through my old neighborhood, right by the mosque.

I had walked hundreds of times in those gardens when I still lived in Paris. And as we walked past the rows of dormant plants—it was November in Paris after all—I spotted her from afar.

A big bush of silver-leafed shiba, shimmering on a gray Parisian day.

We had lived in the same city for a decade, and it took many more years apart for me to finally take note of her when I needed her. I took a clumsy tourist picture with her, teary-eyed from the reunion, squatting like I would in a prison photo, in this colonial garden where she lived in exile. And in the soft bristling of her leaves, a voice saying "Ya benti. I got this, I got this, let it go."

A Small Correction
About Birds and Spoons

IT TURNS OUT THAT IT WASN'T ONLY SPOONS THEY USED TO DIG their way out of the Gilboa prison but pots handles and plates too. It turns out that thirteen days after their miraculous escape, all of them were recaptured by the Occupation forces, and I watch videos of Zacharia Zubeidi and Mahmoud Al-Ardah in a Zionist court, wearing jumpsuits, as people speaking my native language yell at them. It turns out they all received an added five-year sentence to their lifetime of imprisonment.

It turns out that Kai disappeared, was disappeared and that I am left to shove his belongings in trash bags and plastic containers to store in my office. I know that he will never come out again in this lifetime but I hold on to the objects still.

It turns out that I told you earlier that freedom is practiced slowly with determination, and if so, was freedom the few days outside of the jails or will freedom happen after the courtroom, after the trials, after the lives of the six men with the spoons and pot handles are over, after Kai comes back a bird to haunt his tormentors?

I have to ask: Is freedom the hope that they instilled in us, or is freedom the portals of possibilities that open up between the constant catastrophes?

My Mother's Mother

EVERY TIME I BRAID MY HAIR, I THINK ABOUT MY SAFTA AND her own magnificent braid. For as long as I knew her, her hair was gray, except for a patch at the front that was strikingly white. Oh, how I loved this patch! It was the hair of a witch, cascading down her back in a single, perfect braid. An unusual feature that made her short body stand out in a crowd.

As a child I assumed that my Safta's white strand had magical powers; at some point I understood it as a reflection of some deep trauma. On the Internet, people say it's a matter of genetics and vitamin deficiency but I know that stress can have that effect too. The world we live in often lacks poetics. I wonder when the strand turned white. I wonder if it happened when she left her family behind as a child, or if it happened in Marseille, or if it happened in that other camp, they were all sent to when they arrived in the Zionist State. Or maybe it was during one of her many pregnancies.

As a kid, I was fascinated, and slightly terrified by my grandmother. On top of her Moroccan Arabic and Hebrew, she spoke French, a colonial French that I assumed to be tied to class. I imagined her in the French schools of Marrakech, but the reality was that my grandmother left her home country when she was 12. There wasn't that much school in her life.

I would see my grandmother every summer, when my mother would put us on a plane to Tel-Aviv. Like all immigrant families, summer was the time to go back to the village, in our case the depths of the desert of Occupied Palestine. From our home of Mulhouse, the closest international airport was in Basel, half an hour away, but my father would drive us frantically to Zürich because the flights were cheaper there. A few hours in the car, crossing the border to Switzerland as the night turned into day. Always too early, we'd spend hours moving through security, answering intrusive questions. My mother would lead us through the ritual required by immigration services. *Yes, we had packed our own bags. No, we weren't given any wrapped gifts to carry.* My father never traveled with us.

Once in Beer-Sheva, time would slow down to the suffocating halt of my grandmother's house. In her home, days were punctuated by meals, naps, and relatives stopping by. We'd sit around the table, and eat the food of the old country she cooked for us. Matbucha, couscous, shkrena, the foods I imagined her mother preparing for her too. "Eat, eat," was the refrain of those childhood summers, an ancestral act of care that often felt like torment.

But in those early years, I savored those moments with her, the softness of her aging body, the tenderness of her shape. I loved listening to the stories she told, tales of dreams seen as visions. At night, under the cover of the moon, ancestors would visit her and speak languages only the two of them understood, warning her of events to come. The worlds her tongue would draw for us were filled with holy oils, amulets and protections. Hamsa, hamsa, hamsa, her litany against the omnipresent evil eye.

As I grew older, my grandmother would ask me to help her with bathing tasks, and I would go into her tiny bathroom to wash her back. Her hair held up, saturated with conditioner, making way for my sudded hand. She never had any issues being naked in front of me, my grandmother. She had the body of someone who birthed and nursed a lot of children. She made me look tall.

In those years when I started towering over her, her ways became stifling, impossible. Her rigidity couldn't contain the freer ways I learned in my French school and we'd often fight. She couldn't accept my fashion choices and politics, I couldn't accept the rules of her faith. My yearly visits stopped. I would find excuses to stay behind as my mother herded my siblings to the deserts of her youth.

Sometimes, in the early 2010's, my grandmother started chemotherapy and the hair fell out. By that point my visits were rare, prompted by funerals and weddings and it had been a few years since I had seen her, regal in her house dress and luscious hair. But after the chemo, the mythical braid was gone, a slow process I wasn't there to witness. Cancer was devouring her colon, and her most striking feature had to be sacrificed for her survival.

My own mother said that she herself couldn't grow her hair past her shoulders, a limitation I always assumed had to do with the intense straightening routine she was so fond of. Her hair had turned flat and stringy from the hours of pulling and coloring. My mother, who never taught us how to be women, but who could never understand I wasn't one.

I don't have any pictures of my grandmother with her braid, and just thinking about this makes my eyes well up. The only pictures that have survived my many moves and my estrangement from my mother are the one of my grandparents, awkward at my sister's wedding and the one my ex took of them on their way to a family reunion, on my last visit right before I moved to the States.

Two pictures of my grandparents, dressed in their best garments, experiencing deep discomfort in front of the camera.

I remember that day vividly, my sister's wedding. I make a point of not talking about her publicly, since privacy is the only gift I can still offer her. My sister who I can't love without reliving years of trauma; she's the hardest relationship I've ever had to walk away from.

But I can tell you that the day she got married my grandparents came to France, something they only did twice. I can tell you that they stayed with us for a week or two, two Moroccan Jews in Mulhouse, a small post-industrial French city.

Our apartment had turned into a chaotic space, with so many relatives coming from abroad. It felt absurd to have my grandparents in our home; they didn't belong to this landscape. I couldn't wrap my head around them boarding a plane; my grandmother was terrified of escalators. They didn't make sense in our hometown.

In their home, in the desert, my grandparents saw themselves as different than their Arab neighbors. They were Jewish, Mizrahi Jews, not Arabs. In the desert, they held onto the belief, refusing to see the resemblance of their noses and skin tones with that of their non-Jewish neighbors. But outside of the Zionist State, their identities of separation from other North Africans lost all meaning. In Mulhouse, they blended in the large Maghrebi population of our neighbors.

My grandmother looked out of place everywhere she went, slightly confused and nervous. It was summer, but she still looked cold. That wasn't the way I understood her presence in the world. My grandmother was a woman who was in control of the world she lived in. She knew her neighbors, she knew everybody. She had opinions about everything, but in France she was just lost. Her colonial French sounded out of place.

On the day of the wedding, the photograph was taken in front of the reception building and my grandparents are stoically looking at the camera. My grandmother's hair is pulled back.

If you didn't know her, you wouldn't notice my grandmother's slight smirk, the way her mouth is turned and her eyes narrow. I see it and the longing flushes through my body: this is the face of my grandmother's playfulness. This is her playing tricks, sometimes mean-spirited. She would have that face when we played Rummi together and she would cheat. She'd have that face, when she'd throw insults at me, as a joke. When she'd call me a bat kalba (daughter of a dog), or when she'd have hidden meat in my food because being a vegetarian didn't make sense to her. She would have that face when she lied. My grandmother lied a lot.

But I don't have pictures of those moments, and if it weren't for the wedding, I wouldn't even have a picture of the smirk, just whirlwinds of memories that are always present with me. It's the limitation of photography really, that we only get to see what is being photographed.

And there are no pictures of my grandmother, a scarf wrapped around her head, praying over the candles. There are no pictures of her stuffing cash in her bra at the bank in the Old City. There are no pictures of her, wearing her house dress, and her absurdly small slippers sitting in the living room, watching Egyptian soap operas while breaking pieces of food with her right hand.

The last time I saw my grandmother, we spent time together in the cancer ward of Soroka hospital. I sat with her in a little cubicle separated from others by curtains, as the poison that was supposed to save her was being pumped through her body. I remember the walls being yellow, and I remember we took a cab to get there. I remember the ways my grandmother, even in those moments of deep fragility, was still commanding the space of the car, her purse on her lap. "Let me do the talking, the driver will rip you off," she had exclaimed before entering the vehicle, so I sat in silence as she negotiated, chin high.

I am glad there are no pictures of the cancer ward of Soroka hospital. I don't need to relive this moment more than I already do. And I wish I had been better at loving her after that. Once I left, that summer of 2011, I lost contact with her in my rage against my own mother and her own cancer. I lost contact with my grandmother because I had to sever all the ties. I had to leave everybody behind, because my own parents were strangling me, and I didn't know how to escape without scorching the earth around me. I feel deep shame about not being part of my grandmother's life in her last few years. I feel deep shame about not being there to bury her body.

I feel deep shame about not celebrating her life the way she deserved me to. I should have ripped garments to mourn her life, I should have covered mirrors and wept with relatives, sitting in her living room. But I couldn't open that door, I couldn't allow myself to travel back to her house, small shape against my mother's body. I had to exchange my survival for this lifelong shame. And deep down I believe that my grandmother is refusing to come visit my dreams because she's still angry with me. As if I didn't belong in the ancestral thread, as if I didn't deserve such nocturnal presence. I get it, I'm angry with myself too. And I still don't know I had any other choice.

I don't think she would understand the ways my own mother, her own daughter, would cross any boundary, how she would call my employers, message my friends and humiliate me over and over again. And how the only way for me to survive was to disappear.

I'm so sorry about it all Safta, and I am sorry that the only way I can remember you is by looking at old pictures and writing over and over the details of our life together. It's my way of trying to never forget it, it's my way of keeping those fuzzy memories alive, to insist that the blurry images that flash through my head as I think about you stay there and don't disappear. The memories of your dressing table, perfume and lipstick; the memories of our meals, walks and jokes; your hand on my hand, this is all I have.

Remembering you, preserving those moments is my way of rebuilding the bridge I burned.

When I tell people about you, I skip over the moments where you would threaten me with a broom, screaming because you were disgusted I called us aravims. I skip over the parts where my mother learned her stifling ways from you. I skip over the parts where your choices have brought destruction because I have enough understanding of history now to know that you survived camps meant to beat the Zionism into you. I understand that you were told that being an Arab meant renouncing your Jewishness. I understand that you had to justify the loss of home, by validating the existence of the settler-colonial state you were now part of. I understand the ache of leaving your homelands behind and that you would never see your beloved city of Marrakech ever again. I understand that once you crossed the water and transited through Marseille, there was no turning back.

When I tell people about you, I tell them you were a true Capricorn, born the day before Christmas and that it connected you to me, the Christmas baby. I tell them about the food you made, the na3na3 tea you would prepare every morning. I tell them about the ways you named your children the Arabic names of their ancestors who visited you in your dreams. I tell them that all your children changed their names. I tell them about your voice calling for me Ya Benti. I tell them how you never used the Hebrew name my parents gave me and would rather call me "Naima," hard on the ayn. I tell them about your ululations at celebrations, made easier by that one gap in your teeth on the side of your mouth. I tell them about the suitcases full of Nivea cream and French soaps we would bring to you every summer. I tell them about the Egyptian soap operas you would play loudly in the early hours of the day. I tell them about the jewelry made of gold you wore, and your hair. I always tell them about your hair.

I hope that someday you'll forgive me and come back to my dreams Safta, and I hope that when you do it isn't in the stiff clothing of celebrations. I hope that you come to me in your house dress, with your hair braided perfectly down your back. I'll be waiting for you, my hair imperfectly mirroring yours. A cup of tea, a handful of biscuits, maybe in my new home of Philadelphia this time. When we do meet again Safta, I hope you get to tell me everything that I am doing wrong. I hope you insult me for calling myself an Arab and wanting a free Palestine, knowing that I am not a child you can threaten anymore. When you do come see me, Safta, I hope that the night can hold all of our truths spoken in the language of shared colonial pasts, your smirk reflecting the one forming in my eyes.

In the Shadow of His Body

— I. Aftermath —

I GREW UP MY FATHER'S SHADOW, THE SON HE NEVER HAD, THE daughter he named after his father, the queer child he sensed, the vessel of my parents' projections. In my early years, there was nobody else I wanted to be, but him. Back then, I practiced crossing my legs like him, one ankle on my knee, arms spread on the back of the chair, trying to contort into his shape.

But over the years, my body blossomed, shifted. The changes eroded our bond, and slowly we lost our ability to communicate. I am unclear why it became so hard for us, something about my body changing, about me becoming whole outside of his shadow, something about the intensifying violence, about being constantly disappointed, about a shroud being lifted. As I grew older, our early bond turned into an erratic relationship of thunderous conversations, months of silence, followed by short bursts of laughter brought in by our shared interests and similar personalities. After all, in the deeper parts of myself, the ones only I know, it is him I resemble the most. But if I let myself love parts of him, if I let myself remember all the ways that he has shaped me, I worry I will forget the violence of his body that sometimes erupts within mine.

I have not seen my father in over ten years, and will never see my father again. When I left my hometown of Mulhouse, when I left my mother, I left him too.

* * *

In the summer of 1992, when I was seven years old, my father promised me a trip to Pompeii. An adventure of ferries and history and ancient civilizations that me and him could share over my summer break. Until then, every time I traveled was for family: my maternal grandparents in the Zionist State, my mother's sister in Switzerland, my paternal grandmother in Sarre-Union. On paper, I was a well-traveled child, owner of a passport, well-versed in airport etiquette, but in reality I had never gone anywhere that mattered to me. Nor had I, until then, ever traveled with my father: he was the transporter, driving us to the places we needed to be, going home afterwards to go back to work long hours across the border.

Pompeii would be a welcome change, it could open me to a larger world I was craving, with my favorite person. I don't quite know why I was so enamored with Pompeii, but I had probably read about it in a Mickey Mouse or DuckTales strip or maybe in one of the National Geographic issues that accumulated in our bathroom. A civilization frozen in time, a city of the past accessible to our contemporary eyes without any imagination required.

My excitement was fueled by the stories of Tintin and Jules Verne, the same stories that had excited my father when he too was a child. Pompeii, for me, meant that there was life outside of our small town, our small life, our small circle. That the world could be explored, roamed, experienced, instead of constantly feared. Together, we could be adventurers, not just passive observers of others' feats.

I imagined myself coming back to school at the end of the summer, my classmates asking "Where did you go?" only to answer, chest filled with pride, "Pompeii. Papa and I went to Pompeii."

* * *

Four years old, in my bedroom, wearing my favorite black and white onesie, sitting on his back, pretending he's a horse. Six years old, sitting on his shoulders, looking at the world from up in the sky. Eight years old, head on his protruding belly, watching the news. Ten years old, laying down on the couch, bodies mirroring each other, silently reading by his side. Twelve years old, telling him my finger, the one he hit with his open palm, is broken. Twelve years old, watching him cry, telling him, "It's ok, you didn't mean it."

* * *

Mornings didn't exist in our home; our father left before dawn. We woke up to the silence of our sleeping mother, and would quietly get ready, cleaning our rooms before scurrying out of the apartment towards our respective classrooms. Sometimes, we would have enough change to buy ourselves un pain au lait from the schoolyard daily bake sale, but most days we would wait to come home for the lunch of frozen food my mother would have prepared.

Saturdays though would be different. Our father would be there, already awake with a cornucopia of breads bought from the different bakeries he enjoyed. Baguettes and their smaller counterparts ficelle from Barthel, dark loafs from the traditional bakery around the corner. Butter, jam, an assortment of cheese. We would eat our fill before hurrying to our half day at school, knowing we would come home to a slow cooked stew he would have prepared for us.

Sometimes, during the week, I would wake up while the world was still dark, and I would find him hunched over a newspaper, drinking coffee, trying to get ready for his day. I would enter the kitchen and watch him smile at me. "*Qu'est-ce que tu fais debout à cette heure-ci, ma puce?*" In those quiet moments, my father was mine alone.

* * *

Fifteen, his hands wrapped around my ankles angrily pulling me to the ground because I spent some money, his money. Eighteen, his hands dragging my unconscious body towards the ambulance. Twelve, hand in his, walking to the bookstore.

* * *

That summer of 1992, my father and I didn't go to Pompeii. He got laid off from the nuclear plant in Zürich, and there was no money.

Instead of ushering me through this new adventurous era of my life, he took us to Paris, where he fed us tuna cans on church stairs. It was my first time in the capital, a city I would fall in love with a decade later, but this time around, the Haussmanian boulevards disappointed me. Paris felt claustrophobic, a pale replacement for my foray into exploration.

My father never brought Pompeii back, never apologized for not taking me on this trip, and his silence became the terrain of my shame. I knew he was doing his best and I was being ungrateful for wanting more. I was being selfish for wanting something, while he had lost his employment. I wasn't being generous enough; I had to hide my disappointment to carry his feelings instead of my own.

That summer in Paris was the first time I had one of my defining nightmares: somebody is trying to harm me, I try to scream, and my voice is muffled. People I love are around me, but they can't see that I am in danger, that I need them, there is nobody protecting me. Nothing comes out as I open my mouth, I am alone in a sea of familiar faces. I'm under water, or under a pillow and my body feels like it's sinking. I've had thousands of these nightmares over the years, they are still as terrifying as that first time.

That first time in Paris, the dream took place in the long hallway of a metro station and I could see my father a few feet ahead of me but he would not turn around and my voice couldn't reach him. I wet the bed I was sleeping on, in my parent's friend's house by Porte de Clignancourt. A new mattress I had ruined and my father couldn't bring himself to reassure me because he had to pay for that mattress to be replaced with money he didn't have, the money that could have taken us to Mount Vesuvius instead. I was left alone with my shame.

* * *

His booming voice calling us for dinner, " À table!." His jaw twitching before he hits me. His hands turning into fists when startled. His tears listening to a requiem on his father's Yahrzeit. His body falling to the ground during one of their fights. His fingers strumming his guitar. His legs crossed on the ground as he reorganizes his bookshelves. His arms open wide as he smokes a Gitane on the balcony, my small child body imitating his.

* * *

Things we shared: A love of music, a quiet introversion, a sense of humor, an intense aversion to authority figures, a fondness for animals, a love of good food, coffee and cigarettes, anarchist politics, constant rebellion.

* * *

Sometime in my early twenties, my father came to visit me in Paris, where I had moved at the age of eighteen. The memory feels like an anomaly, this wasn't something that happened to us, my father never came to my apartment on avenue de Choisy, a tiny and crooked place above a Chinese restaurant that I lived in for most of my undergrad years. We weren't able to be alone back then. But here he is in my memory, here we are, walking through the Sentier, the old Jewish ghetto, before crossing rue de Rivoli and making our way to the Mémorial de la Shoah, right before the river, a place I have never been to until now. Knowing who we were back then, I am assuming that he is walking with a limp, too slowly for my urban impatience; I am assuming that I am frustrated with him, his jokes, his habit of haranguing strangers. I am assuming he is poking at me, enjoying his ability to rouse me.

The next part of the memory makes more sense. We enter the Mémorial de la Shoah, a freshly inaugurated building, a new location for my father to continue his obsessive quest of retracing his lineage, trying to access some history of his people. Here we are in the memory, walking past the security guard, me opening my purse for its contents to be examined, both of us walking through the metal detector that always signals a Jewish space in France. And then, here we are again, me and my father, alone in the courtyard of this memorial, here we are looking at the wall of names, the list of the 76,000 Jewish people who were deported from France by the Vichy government to die in the gas chambers of Auschwitz, Sobibor, and Majdanek.

And here he is, my father, collapsed on the floor, wailing in the middle of the courtyard. Fernand Keim, his name, buried amongst the columns of death, engraved in the stone.

———

— 0: A REPETITION —

"[…] it is this sharing and understanding of the experience of meaninglessness that is in and of itself healing. For what can one say after Auschwitz?"

* * *

On August 13th 1943, my grandfather André Keim and his father Fernand are arrested by the Gestapo in the house at 39 rue des Voileurs in Blâmont, Meurthe-et-Moselle where they have been living since escaping their ancestral home of Struth, Bas-Rhin in France. The two of them are transferred to the internment camp des Écrouves, where over 4,000 people will transit throughout the Holocaust.

On October 28th 1943, my great-grandfather Fernand Keim is placed on convoy #61 that leaves the train station of Paris-Bobigny at 10:30 am with one thousand Jewish people in it, according to a telegram sent by Aloïs Brunner, Adolf Eichmann's right-hand man. The convoy follows its usual itinerary: Paris-Bobigny, Épernay, Châlons-sur-Marne, Bar-le-Duc, Novéant, Metz, Saarbrücken, Mannheim, Frankfurt am Main, Erfurt, Engelsdorf Mitte (Leipzig), Dresden, Görlitz, Neisse (Nysa), Cosel, before arriving in Auschwitz 53 hours later.

Convoy #61 arrives at Auschwitz-Birkenau on October 30th 1943. 284 men are selected into forced-labor and tattooed with numbers 159546 to 159829. The next day, on October 31 1943, 103 women are selected into forced-labor and tattooed with numbers 66451 to 66553. The 613 remaining people are brought into the gas chamber where they die of Zyklon B asphyxiation before being cremated. Fernand Keim is recorded to have died in Auschwitz Birkenau on November 2nd 1943. He is 66 years old.

* * *

Sarah Keim née Caron is arrested from the house at 39 rue des Voileurs in Blâmont, Meurthe-et-Moselle where she had been living since she escaped her home of Struth, Bas-Rhin with her husband and middle child. She is transferred to the camp des Écrouves, on 13 July 1944. Sarah Keim née Caron dies on 24 July 1944. She is 63 years old.

André Keim is liberated from the internment camp des Écouvres on August 31st 1944, five days before his thirty-second birthday.

* * *

In the winter of 1952, André's only child is born. He names him Fernand.

* * *

On April 20th 1978, André Keim dies of a heart attack in the hospital of Saverne, Bas-Rhin, 20 miles from his home of Sarre-Union. He is 65 years old.

* * *

In the winter of 1984, two days after his thirty-second birthday, Fernand's second child is born. He names them Noam Andrée.

* * *

At the time of writing this essay, my father, Fernand is still alive. He is 71 years old.

———

— ∞: Eruptions —

"Earth may be unique among the planets in the solar system in that its outer rigid skin, the crust and lithosphere is continuously being destroyed and regenerated. It has active plate tectonics, where the heat and smoke of volcanism rise from the two main battlefields between the plates: the rifts or ocean ridges and the subduction zones. The most important consequence of plate tectonics is geologic recycling of materials, turning the Earth into an immense chemical factory where volcanism plays a crucial role."

Mount Vesuvius, lies on the Gulf of Naples, five miles east from the city, a short jaunt from the shore. It is known as a somma-stratovolcano, meaning that it was born from the remnants of Mount Somma 17,000 years ago and acquired its conical shape over millennia, one layer of lava at a time, each eruption adding to its build, until it reached its current height of 4000 feet.

Like all volcanoes, Mount Vesuvius is the result of frictions, tectonic plates moving, creating pockets of gas under the surface of the Earth that need to be released in the form of eruptions.

There have been 54 reported eruptions of Mount Vesuvius during the Holocene period, the last one occurring in the spring of 1944.

But its most famous eruption is the one that happened on a fall day of 79 AD, destroying the cities of Pompeii and Herculaneum, or more accurately, entombing them in thick layers of ashes over the course of two days.

A Plinian eruption is what experts call this type of volcanic activity: a violent explosion, an outburst of gas-rich magma, resembling a giant rocket blast shooting vertically upward, projecting tephra miles from the caldera. An eruption named after Pliny the Elder who died in the explosion, as recounted by his nephew Pliny the Younger in letters sent to the historian Tacitus, some twenty-five years later, likening the cloud of destruction to the stone pine, one of the Roman empire's most famous symbol:

"The cloud could best be described as more like an umbrella pine than any other tree, because it rose high up in a kind of trunk and then divided into branches. I imagine that this was because it was thrust up by the initial blast until its power weakened and it was left unsupported and spread out sideways under its own weight. Sometimes it looked light coloured, sometimes it looked mottled and dirty with the earth and ash it had carried up."

It is an unusual type of eruption, far away from the popular culture images of viscous lava running down the slopes of volcanoes, a particularly violent one, too fast to be escaped, trapping humans into their forthcoming death.

On that fall day of 79 AD, Vesuvius covered the city of Pompeii under a 16 foot blanket of ash. Hot, smoldering tephra and ash fell onto the city and the city's inhabitants, bodies, objects and buildings were imprinted onto their grim, ghastly casts, creating what we know as the archeological site and tourist attraction of Pompeii. Perfectly captured snapshot of a dying city.

Every year, over 2 million tourists walk the streets of the former city of Pompeii, hoping to catch a glimpse of life 2000 years ago, seemingly perfectly frozen in time, captured forever.

———

— 2: A calcification —

There isn't much I know about my father's family before the war; everything I gleaned, I gleaned from the genealogy websites I have been using after leaving him. I blame myself for not listening carefully enough when I was younger, for not remembering the details shared during meals and gatherings; I know a lot of my ignorance is my fault alone and now it is too late.

Everything I learned from the generations before my grandparents' are names and dates and addresses but what I craved were stories, traditions, rituals, impossible to gather without human interaction.

I grew up jealous of friends who had attics filled with family heirlooms passed down from generations before them. Because I had never seen the homes where my parents had grown up, because by the time I was born, belongings were limited. Because people who flee do not get to pack, because people who are persecuted do not get to keep what matters to them.

In my paternal grandmother's apartment, there were a few remnants of this grandfather I never met whose name I shared. A picture of André, his bed, an old cane, his Yellow Star, a box of pictures.

In the attic, my grandmother kept his documents, unceremoniously thrown into cardboard boxes, letters he had sent to the French government, detailing his torture in the camp des Écrouves. Suing them for a pension. I must have been seven or eight; I imagined the scenes he described, images of him being denied his prosthetics, forced to crawl. Now I wonder how he avoided death.

Downstairs, in the cabinet, in the shelf below the Merveilles du Monde chocolate Grand-Mère would buy for our visits, a small box shaped like a trunk, filled with pictures of family members, black and white mementos of generations past. Sometimes, on the back, a few words written in ink, telling us whose body was memorialized; "Mort à Auschwitz" becoming the chorus of our trauma song. Children and elders, kept in a small box in a widow's cabinet.

Now I wonder how the box of pictures survived the end of his world, I wonder who hid them and where, for them to be in my grandmother's cabinet decades later.

I often looked at those pictures as a child, on my way to the chocolate or her scarves I'd wrap myself in, but, as always, my memory fails me and the only picture I can see with clarity is the one of my grandfather, sitting on the cabinet, staring at us, large features that remind me of his son's, bald, clean shaven, proud, without a smile to be seen.

* * *

I cannot think of a time in my life when I wasn't aware of the annihilation of my ancestors, when I didn't know about my father's father, about his survival, about his larger than life presence that overshadowed ours, even after his death. About this mythical man who had lost both of his legs, walked with two canes, and continued to raise and sell cattle and drive a car.

At the age of three, I would stand in the yard of my preschool and talk to him, reverently. André. At the age of three, I had already mastered fear, and knew how to behave around his memory. Small, polite, quiet. I'd talk to him every time I would fall off the wooden train in the schoolyard, every time the blood would rush out of my nose, a common occurrence. I would never look up, but I would move energy up, telling him about my day, hoping he would forgive me for the fall off the wooden train and the blood rushing out of my nose. I understood every failure as danger. They said I was too quiet, too shy, that I never made a sound. I wonder if the silence was the voice of my constant fear.

* * *

His beloved cows. His admiration of the Géneral de Gaulle. His belief that a day without work is a wasted day. His twin bed, pushed against his wife's. His mouth, filled with Alsatian curses.

* * *

My father was born the miracle baby of two people who had lost legs and family and youth during the war. He was to embody everything they had lost or maybe, simply be a source of joy after the impossible darkness. The birth was difficult, and required a slash through his mother's belly, another mutilation, and when he emerged he had two lobes attached to his left ear, flesh shaped like a duck's beak that I would caress in my early years as I sucked my thumb.

Stories about his childhood confused me; the world he had grown up in seemed small, constricting, at odds with the man with a foreign wife, foreign children, foreign life. The man who sang The Clash and had worn his hair long before losing it, the man who sported a wild, unruly beard, the man who, faithfully, voted for the Communist party every election, who loved John Fante and Arthur Rimbaud, who bought me copies of *Johnny's Got a Gun* and *A Confederacy of Dunces*, who taught me about Third Worldism and Black Liberation. The stories of his childhood told a different version of him.

Fernand was born only seven years after the war ended, in a family of farmers. His father was a cattle merchant tending to the land with his brothers in the small town of Sarre-Union, in this portion of Alsace nicknamed bossue, as in hunched, because of the soft humps of the land.

A land at the border, constantly shifting hands between Germany and France, the first slice of land that felt the tremor of the Nazi occupation.

Fernand was supposed to follow the familial footsteps, learn about the plants and the bees and the trees of this land only ten miles away from Struth, where André was born, where his father's father was born, where they had lived for generations before the war. But something shifted.

Early on, at ten maybe, my father left his rural hometown for the city of Strasbourg, a move that would effectively disconnect him from his ancestors' rituals and traditions.

Fernand went to a boarding school in the city of Strasbourg, only a few hours away from his home but far enough that he would only see his parents on weekends and holidays. A school built after the war for orphans who had lost their families in the camps or the chaos, l'ORT was designed to professionalize those young Jewish children, to give them technical skills, so that they could support themselves. There, my father learned to become an electrician, a profession he still practiced in my youth. My grandmother alluded to regular fist fights and bad grades, to time in the wrestling team to tame him.

My mother, during my parents' daily fights, would often reference l'ORT as proof that he was unlovable. How else do you explain parents shipping you out at such a young age? Sometimes, she would slightly shift the angle, telling him that his behavior was the result of his genetics, his parents' disability, the result of unfit parents who had chosen a better path for him by giving him away.

Regardless, my father spent his adolescence in a trauma capsule, surrounded by children and adults also scarred by the war. I have known plenty of men who grew up in confined spaces, I know what happens there; I understand that there are things my father probably never talked about, that he never will. And yet he spoke about his time there somewhat fondly, much more so than his time at home.

My father, the largest person in our household, would shrink before my eyes, describing time spent with his own father: stories of chores, rigid rules, explosive anger. He had a lot of shoes to fill, he who was supposed to bring back to life his father's father; he who was supposed to embody the legacy of his grandfather, a man idealized, who died in the most impossible way. It seemed that no matter what he tried to do, he couldn't meet the expectations of his father. My father taught me that there is a traumatized boy in every violent man I encounter.

* * *

The satchel in which he kept every remnant of cigarettes he smoked in case of another war. The apple he ate in the dark every night before bed. His canes used as weapons against an antisemitic school employee. His expectation of food on the table whenever he was ready. His yelling at his son, Fernand, on Saturday morning to come do his chores instead of reading.

* * *

When I entered my father's life, he had already been living in the Zionist State for some fifteen years, having migrated to the desert at the age of seventeen with classmates, under the promise of advanced training and work opportunities. He didn't speak Hebrew; he didn't know anybody there and yet he made a life. I don't know of any seventeen-year-olds who leave happy families; I imagine my father needed room to grow, away from his parents' trauma. A family cycle.

* * *

A memory: I am four or five years old, big light brown eyes shining in the middle of my face, dark hair cut in a bob, playing on the tiled floor of our living room. I trace the arabesque that moves from one tile to the other with my fingers , completing a shape, mesmerizing curves of dark blue against an Earth colored background. I am lost in my own head, unaware of my surroundings; I am an imagination child. On the table of dark green marble sits one of my father's few prized possessions: a crystal ashtray that belonged to his father, a beautiful heavy round piece of glass, carved out to refract light, intimidating in both its shape and symbolism. An object I know not to touch. Somehow, in the midst of my silent game, my child's arm knocks the ashtray off the table and it lands on the hard floor, glass hitting ceramic, shattering in enough pieces that it is destroyed.

Instantly my body tightens, preparing for my father to run into the room and erupt, my torso hardens in anticipation of the intense anger that will come crashing on my small body. Over thirty years later, I can conjure the pressure building up within me, the energy accumulating towards uncontrollable tears, that half a second of waiting that has lived in my body forever.

My father enters the room, big-boned and tall, and I look at him terrified at what will happen next, looking for the cues in his face and body. He looks down disappointed, starts picking up the pieces off the floor, turns to me and says "It's ok, you didn't mean it."

* * *

When my grandfather died in a hospital twenty miles away from his home, when my grandfather's heart gave up, my father wasn't there. He was away from the land of his ancestors, away from his father. I don't know that he ever forgave himself.

———

3- An echo

"Your grandfather lives inside your heart."

As has become the habit, I am on the phone with the ancestral healer, trying to reconnect the dots of my lineage. We start like we always do, with them asking me "Do you have any questions you want to ask your guides today?" as I try to gather my thoughts, usually jotted down on the notebook labeled, "Somatics, genealogy." Today, the pages have stayed blank. I am not sure I am ready to ask, I am scared of what I could learn during this call.

"Well, I've been thinking a lot about my paternal grandfather. He was an Alsatian Jew, survived the war, lost his legs and both his parents, and died before I was born. My parents gave me his name, André, and I have always wondered about our relationship, because…you know, it's a big deal. You know, carrying his legacy and stuff. I have always wondered why they gave me the name of a man who I never met, who would probably hate me. You know, as I make my family tree, all the records that come up are of his ancestors, and I have no connection to any of that lineage. Like, I even learned that…What is it? his great-uncle, Théophile, crossed the Atlantic and lived in Philadelphia, and was buried there. I feel like my grandfather is trying to tell me something. I can't fucking figure out why just yet."

I have just spent a day driving around my newly-discovered ancestors' former homes in Philadelphia, taking pictures of what, in the last century, has turned into abandoned lots and new buildings, trying to feel something as I placed a stone on Théophile's grave. I have been combing census records, and lists of Jews, trying to find details that would humanize any of them.

André's lineage is the only one of my tree that is documented: Alsatian Jews who tended to the land and peddled, and changed nationality as the border crossed them. Ancestors who tie me to a land that I left as soon as I possibly could, a land in which I was always made to feel out of place, unwanted, foreign, un.e sale juif.ve, un.e sale arabe.

And yet, a small part of my body was connected to this land and André kept returning to my mind. The only one of my grandparents who died in the land of his ancestors. A man who died of a heart attack five years before I was born, a man I only knew from exactly two black and white pictures. A man whose violence lived in the body of his son. A man whose trauma lives in mine too. A man I have never wanted to love.

"Anything else you want me to know before I ask your guides?"

"No, that's it."

"Ok, great. I'm going to call them, give me a few minutes."

The line goes silent, and I try to focus on my breath, noticing the way it catches within my chest, how hard it is for me to stay in the anticipation of this moment. What does my grandfather want to tell me, what if he tells me that he doesn't care for me? What if he tells me he recognizes himself in me?

"So, the first image that's coming is just showing that your grandfather is connected to you very directly through the, like, the bottom.. hmm..like tip of your heart, your actual physical heart. Hmmm like they're just showing kind of the left and the right ventricle together like the bottom, like, just the bottom piece, as if you could kind of carve out a little triangle at the bottom of your heart. And that is like, directly where you and your grandfather connect."

The certitude shocks me. André lives in my heart.

* * *

When André died of a heart attack in the spring of 1979, he had spent half of his life grieving the death of a life: his parents, his home, his joy, his belief that there was hope in this world, the healing that had sustained him before the war. When he died, my parents hadn't even met yet, and I am not sure what either of their lives even looked like then. But I do know about grief and despair, and I do know about my father's body on the couch, every year on April 20th listening to his requiems, crying, and the way all of us knew not to approach him, then.

And I do know that, throughout my childhood, my father who did not care about religious rituals, who ate ham and salami, and hid food in his trunk during Yom Kippur, that same man would volunteer at our synagogue, to wash the bodies of men who had died, that he would volunteer to sit for minyan, so that Kaddish could be recited, so that their bodies could be properly buried. So that their death could be witnessed and remembered.

———

4- A healing

A history: On February 14, 1349, there was another hell, another moment that ended lives and shattered legacies. On the heels of the Black Plague ravaging Europe, rumors of the wells being poisoned by Jews were spread across the city of Strasbourg by the guilds. The resentment against Jews was already brewing then, accelerated by their role as money lenders, one of the few positions allowed by law for people of their faith.

On February 14, 1349 they were burned alive, hundreds of men, women and children engulfed by flames, until all that was left was the smell of charred bones and destruction. The few who agreed to convert were spared. When the hysteria died down, they proclaimed the edict that forbade them to live within the city limits forcing Alsatian Jews to live in rural communities, like the estate of La Petite Pierre that would become the village of Struth where André ancestors settled with a few other families as early as 1756. They weren't allowed to own land, they weren't allowed much, so like most Alsatian Jews they'd survive the poverty inflicted on their people through commerce.

And in the hearts of André's ancestors, Fernand's ancestors, my ancestors, despair started building up, a wound of historical proportions that would fill their bodies for generations to come. Who are we when hope disappears?

* * *

A litany: André, who were you before the torture? What parts of yourself did you lose at the end of your world?

André, why did you choose to live in my heart? Why did you choose to dwell in the most sacred part of me? Was it to protect or was it to witness? Are you the reason why I never feel like the body I live in is the body of my mind?

André, why did you choose to live in my heart? Did you want to be there to expel the pain that you knew would live at the center of me? Did you want to make up for the errors of your son, shaped by the ways you shaped him?

André, why did you choose to live in my heart? Did you know that if you stayed in this heart of mine, that if you whispered, you'd be able to remind me of the young me, the me that would ask for a telescope for my birthday, the me that would set it on the river banks and stare at the mallards until my eyes blurred from the shine of their feathers?

André, did you want me to carry on your legacy? Did you want me to heal, or did you want to heal me? Did you believe that if you stayed long enough I would get it? Did you believe that someday I'd finally understand that it is in the complexity that we all exist, that no matter the amount of documentation, we are all fragments, figments to be put back together as a full story. André, is that it? André, how old are you in my heart? Are you me or am I you?

André, do you love me? The child who was never a girl and never a boy. The child who still can't feel their chest, even when they know it is where you live, a firefly in my left ventricle, fluttering around.

* * *

Sometimes, I wonder what would have happened to my relationship with my father if we had taken that trip to Pompeii. Would a trip to the Gulf of Napoli make up for the generations of trauma living in our bodies? The ancestral threads of despair that we both have had to contend with? Would it have been enough to forgive him for the violence, the disappointment, the shame?

I am sure that if my father had taken me to Pompeii, I would still have had that dream of losing my voice. I would still wake up feeling ashamed of my inability to escape danger, I would still feel shame about my voice failing me. I would still believe myself alone in the world, when really, this hasn't been the case since I left him, her, them. But the dream isn't about me and this life, is it?

And yet, if my father had taken me to Pompeii, I would also have had the memories of seeing preserved remnants of civilization that should have been completely wiped out. Of miracles. Of promises kept. Of my father showing up for me. If he had taken me to Pompeii, maybe I would have forgiven him more, on account of the new memories we would have created together.

And even if he hadn't taken me to Pompei, if he had held my childhood disappointment with his two hands, if he had been the adult for once, I might have been able to extend more generosity. I would have trusted his intentions, his commitment to my joy.

But what I really needed from my father was for him to hold my shame before it spread and hardened within me. If my father had taught me that the igneous rock that holds my center wasn't mine to carry, if he had taught me that the Sisyphean task wasn't mine but his, theirs, maybe there wouldn't be this tear at the center of me. If he had prevented the lava of shame from spreading, if he had prevented the calcification, the new shape, maybe we would have been able to share the shape of vulnerability, of heavy legacies and broken cycles.

If he had prevented the calcification, we could still be sharing a bond, a different one, one of safety and trust. One in which he sits at my side and hears about my life on the other side of the ocean he never crossed; he would be able to see all the ways I am still of his body. He would be able to see that, yes, his dreams and mine were always intertwined. He would see that I still sit the way he did, maybe does, one ankle on my knee, arms spread on the back of the chair.

And what if, instead of a rock, my father had planted a seed to bloom? What if my father had loved me so much that his love for me had brought him hope and possibility? *Avec des si, on mettrait Paris en bouteille*, with a litany of ifs, we could shove Paris into a bottle.

After all these years, I have never made it to the Gulf of Napoli, I have never seen the remnants of Pompeii, unsure of what to do with this dream that was ours, or maybe only mine all along? Would a ferry ride make up for generations of despair and disappointment?

* * *

A story: André is sitting on a stool in the barn of his family farm, his feet barely touching the ground. He is six years old, tending to one of the cows who has been sick. The smell of hay permeates the room, the air is filled with buzzing pollinators and the blinding light of a spring sun ray.

Guenendel is the 4th generation of her family to be born in this barn, to be tended to by a Keim and there is a certitude in André's hands that comes from being of the land of the people who birthed him. His father has taught him some techniques to help the cattle and it's time for him to try them, see if he will be any good at following his father's footsteps.

André moves his hand against her bovine body, fingers going up and down as if he was milking her. Closely, he listens to what her muscles and blood and bones are saying to him, closely he notices the disease, the infection, inching away from her insides, ready to erupt to the surface. André learns of his gift, golden child. On that day, he learns that is able to heal the mammals growing on his land, with the might of his own body. André's heart fills with pride replacing our lineage's despair with joy.

Freedom Trees

LATE SPRING AND EARLY SUMMER BELONGS TO THE DELICATE smell of lindens in bloom, covering the stench of violence and death in the city of Philadelphia. Every year, as the temperatures rise, so does the litany of guns at night, the refrain of a city intent on breaking your heart. Never enough branches and trunks to cover the cries.

In the dramatic sun of a Philadelphia spring morning, I walk one mile east from my home to my office without the shade of a tree. My body hasn't adjusted yet to the cruelty of their absence; I grew up under the cover of linden trees lining up our boulevards and populating the parks of my childhood. Trees I have always known as *tilleul* in my French home. In this new life, under the canopy of the American Empire, trees only grow where money lives. Halfway through the walk, across the street from an encampment of tents, three linden saplings dig their roots into the cement; three green islands in a sea of gray trying to nurture the sidewalk into a different story. I wonder if the linden trees growing in the sidewalk can grow roots deep enough to survive this world.

At the end of the walk, I will open the front gate, sit on my chair and listen to people's stories of grief and torture inside and outside prisons. Marcus's eldest son died last week, his youngest sits in a jail for a death at the hand of a gun. David lost a cousin and Debra's niece died too. Michelle calls me from the hallway of the penitentiary that confines her. I listen, give advice, help make plans on how to move forward. Sometimes, joyful news. Shyeed is having another baby, his smile illuminating the room. *You want some candy Miss Noam*, he'll ask, shifting his boyish frame in the chair. We'll laugh together. *Remember that time we sat in the probation building for two hours?* He'll make jokes out of minuscule moments, making the day easier to bear. His visits, inconsistent, feel like a burst of life in otherwise gloomy days.

When he leaves, I will be alone in the building until I can't listen anymore, and I will walk home, one mile west under a quieter sun, stopping by the young lindens again.

In my former life, I took the lindens for granted, never paying attention to them closely, but on this walk home I will be grateful. Engulfed in despair, heavy from a broken heart, I stop and caress their tender heart-shaped leaves. I stop on the sidewalk to touch their bark, yelping at the first tuft of late-spring flowering. There is life growing on the sidewalk, there will be hope.

* * *

In Poland, they believed the linden to be so holy that they would name a calendar month after the tree. While in French and English, July is named after Roman Emperors, in Polish, they call it *lipiec*, after the linden tree they call *lipa*. The Slavic people believed that the linden witnessed and purified its surroundings and planted the tree next to the grave of those who died. Sometimes, they still plant a tree to commemorate the birth of a child. The tree marking the time of life passed.

* * *

As I have settled into life on Turtle Island, I had to relearn the names of all plants and animals in my new language, and somehow can never connect them to their European counterparts. They're stored in a new part of my brain, isolated from any knowledge of the natural world I had in French. I do not understand the *tilleul* of my childhood to be related to the linden. I do not understand the nettles that grow in my garden to be the *orties* of my childhood, I do not understand the dandelions to be the *pissenlits* we'd play with as children, and the sparrows aren't *moineaux* anymore. It all feels like a different realm, my brain divided in two.

In the American mind I inhabit most days, if I think of a *moineau*, my mind goes blank. No images of the birds I lived with for most of my life, no tiny body hopping on the cobblestone streets of my youth. As if my brain needed a clean slate to get acquainted with a new environment, as if I needed to forget where I came from to become anew. I'll mumble words in French and realize I do not know what they mean in English. I'll use softwares to translate *ragondin* and *badiane*, learning that they are the nutrias and star anises of my new life.

* * *

I read somewhere that the linden is the oldest tree of Europe, resisting all the plagues that have afflicted its counterparts. They say that there are Lithuanian lindens that are 2,500 years old. In Lithuania, they call the linden *liepa*. The Lithuanian *liepas* trees were alive when Socrates drank the poison of the hemlock, the Lithuanian liepas trees were alive when Siddharta Gautama attained salvation under the sacred fig tree. I long to touch their oversized limbs and listen to the story they tell. I want to know what they have learned from watching worlds end; I want them to teach me how to survive. I don't know what the American mind makes of the linden but the absence of trees in the city fills my lungs with the loss of worlds fully-known. Will I ever come close enough to the American linden?

* * *

In France, we believe the lindens to be trees of love, and French cafes will serve you linden tea, *un thé au tilleul* to soothe a heavy heart. I didn't know that linden was *tilleul* until I did, and it felt reassuring to reconnect with an old friend on the sidewalk of Philadelphia. The close cousin of an old friend. A younger sibling, lacking the majesty of their European counterpart. *Tilia americana* and *Tilia europeana* in their botanical names, the solution to my fragmented brain. But sometimes the botanical names of plants aren't poetic enough for the stories I am trying to tell.

The French *tilleuls* haven't been around for that long, but they too tell stories. In the last year of the 16th century, the king Henry IV appointed the Duke de Sully to the higher court. Now, grand commissioner of highways, Sully went on to plant trees across the kingdom. Lindens and elms were brought in front of the villages' churches to provide shade and a space for the villagers to deal with the matters of their community at the dusk of the Thirty years war. A new agora, under the heart-shaped leaves of linden and elm trees to rekindle a fragile unity. *Tilleuls et ormes.* They'd call them *Arbres de Sully*, for the man who gave the order to plant them as if trees belonged to humans instead of the reality that we are all made of trees. Over the centuries the trees battered by storms, hail, and thunder would find their limbs split. Some of them are currently held by metal plates to survive the harshness of their old age, deformed by their experiences of time.

A couple centuries after they planted the Sully trees, after the people ended the monarchy with a revolution, they planted the linden trees (the *tilleuls*, really) to symbolize the freedom ringing all over the territory. Two centuries later, in 1989, the French government would plant 36,000 trees to commemorate the freedom the French people had acquired through sweat and tears. One for each town of the Republic that used to be a monarchy, named *arbre de la Liberté* as in freedom trees. I was four years old then, already in school and there must be a memory involving the planting of our own freedom tree, the *Marseillaise* sung in unison, but the fragments feel like stories told rather than lived experiences. The Lithuanian *liepas* by then would have been giants, older than most of their fellow timber friends. There are no direct synonyms for tree in both French and English, and the lack of options breaks my heart but I know our lindens to be prophets of freedoms hard acquired.

* * *

It is easy to identify a linden tree. Its leaves are perfect heart shapes of dark green tinted with blue. Symbols of love and good luck to the Germans, protecting us from the evil spirits to the Poles.

In the primeval forest of Bialowieza in Poland, the last remaining forest that still somewhat looks like forests should without human destruction, there is a large contingent of linden trees amongst the oaks and ashes, spruces and pines. *Chênes, frênes, épicéas et pins.* Old trees nestled in the northwestern part of the country, spilling over our imaginary borders to Belarus. Three packs of wolves live in the forest along with bison, wild boars, roe, otters, cranes, storks, and four owl species.

They've been there for so long, they have seen centuries unfold, the giants of Bialowieza. Safe from destruction because the land belonged to royalty for so long. Bialowieza, the forest that stood tall as almost all Polish Jews were exterminated; Bialowieza a metaphor for freedom from the ravages of our capitalist civilizations, only 75 miles east of the Treblinka death camp. They don't know for sure how many people died in Treblinka, but they estimate it at eight hundred thousand. Eight hundred thousand people gone behind the cover of barbed wires and pine branches. Once the destruction was total they dismantled the buildings, the barbed wires and pine branches and planted a forest of spruces and pines on top of the ashes of the dead. If only the Polish *lipas* could have protected their lives. If only the spruces and pines could bring back eight-hundred thousand back to life.

My grandfather's father died amongst the Polish trees; he perished in Auschwitz. He was an Alsatian Jew and the trees didn't save him. But on the other side of my father's tree, my grandmother's mother and father who grew up amongst the Polish *lipas* found safety away from their home on a path illuminated by the fires of pogroms. If they had still been in Poland when the genocide became systematized, they would have been closer to the Janiszew concentration camp anyway, a stone throw away from a young Esther Krinitz, hiding amongst the birches.

* * *

In the middle of the winter of 2020, I had taken a train down to Baltimore, to get a tattoo from a queer whose work I admired. I had asked them to draw a mystical goddex of the forest, depicting the interconnectedness of the moss, fungi and trees because I needed to believe in something bigger than me. My leg still tender and wrapped in plastic, I walked a few miles to the American Visionary Museum, killing time before my train back. Amongst their general collection of folk art, they were exhibiting *Esther and the Dream of One Loving Human Family*, an installation of large tapestries, made by a quiet Maryland seamstress named Esther Krinitz.

Like my ancestors, Esther also had to leave her home of Poland, and she embroidered 36 panels of fabric to describe the story of her survival and the loss of her family and community to the Nazi horrors. She was twelve then and in 36 delicate tapestries embroidered with childish characters and whimsical details, she told the story of her world engulfed in death. She depicted the progressive destruction of their traditions, the walk towards death of her shtetl. In the panels she exquisitely embroidered, she portrays herself a child running away from her family, hiding in the Polish forests to avoid death. The panels are covered in trees: birch, pine, cherry. *Bouleaux, pins, cerisiers.* No lindens, but Polish trees that sheltered her body. The birch trees that saved her life.

In my mind her forest and Bialowieza meld, one canopy of protection against genocide. I imagined the Bialowieza forest, I imagined people hiding, I imagined myself tripping over branches, and the way my body responded told me that, inside of me there were people who had to experience safety amongst the trees. I have known for a long time the ways my body crumples and shakes when I enter deep woods; I know that sometimes I am transported into nervous systems that aren't mine. I am aware that deserts bring me peace and forests arouse me in ways that feel maddening. In my mind the forest didn't bring my people protection, the forest swallowed them. What happened to my people in the forests? How many of my people hid like Esther under the trees? Did they survive?

* * *

I first read about the Bialowieza forest in Richard Power's *Overstory* in the summer of 2020. I borrowed it from the library, and devoured it, hungry for the landscape it depicted. I imagined myself part of the cast of characters trying to save old-growth forests from being destroyed. I wondered what it would take for me to match their bravery.

That summer, as I read about forests and worlds without humans, we had been confined inside our home because of the plague that was ravaging the world. Not the first plague for the trees to witness but the first one of my lifetime. We sat in our home, working from our computers. I didn't walk a mile east to my office anymore, the stories of torture and grief entered my home instead. Clarence died inside the penitentiary that had confined him for half a century. Dante got sick and barely made it out alive. Marcus lost another family member. Michelle got out and was arrested again.

We bought extenders so that the internet could reach corners it couldn't before. We wiped down the groceries, and practiced new forms of socialization over screens and phones. The only way to travel that felt safe was to drive to cabins around Pennsylvania and walk around the woods. Johnny and I would go see trees, lots of them. We'd walk amongst the tulip poplars and the hemlocks and I would experience fright and awe all at once. *Tulipiers de Virginie et pruches.*

Every moment spent in these forests turned into state parks, found me digging deeper and deeper into the well of destruction that is held by the American empire. Only an estimated 1% of the forests that existed before the brutal colonization of the land still exist on the East Coast and on our drives, I would imagine the lost forests engulfing us. If only the American trees could reclaim this land. If only the linden trees could reforest themselves.

* * *

Do you ever play the game of walking through an American city and wondering what the land looked like before? Do you ever feel like the asphalt of an American sidewalk is too new to not have been a marsh a heartbeat ago? I miss the sidewalks of cities that existed before we killed the forests of this world, the Paris and Marseille, *Lutèce et Massalia*, cities that have seen empires fall. I feel the memories of lands past under my feet, and I want them to topple the cement over and seed worlds.

Because the lindens were here before the Empire and there were communities and societies who already knew. Who knew better than to cut all the trees. The Iroquois, the Erie, the Cherokee, the Micmac, the Ojibwa, the Pawnee, the Chippewa people and many more I don't know would make medicinal use of the linden. As a remedy for diarrhea, and as cough medicine. They'd use the soft linden bark for furniture, to build canoes and to make ropes.

Because, after the Empire, after they built this country with the blood of African men and women, the trees would shelter bodies escaping to freedom. The loblolly pines, hickories and oaks protecting the Moses of her time as she walked her people from Maryland to the freedom awaiting them in Philadelphia. *Les pins tadéa, caryers et chênes.*

* * *

What would it take for the lindens of Philadelphia to witness one more collapse? Are they already doing so? In the summer of 2020, I was living in the heart of the imploding empire. Empire is the same in French. *L'empire*, with a pun *l'an pire*, the worst year.

In Philadelphia, we were protesting the constant death of Black men at the hands of the police and the helicopters were constantly buzzing over our house, as we watched the world join us in grief. Massive crowds swarming the streets to demand freedom, columns of young Black men asking to be heard in their dignity. An empire in one of its worst years trying to reckon with its worst years, its foundation of racial capitalism built on genocides; an empire in one of its worst years trying to move through the grief never named collectively. An empire in one of its worst years trying to recognize the roots of its violence, the legacy of destruction.

During the long weeks of the much-needed uprising, as we tried to survive the plague, we were surrounded by police, explosions of fireworks and of ATMS, constant sirens, and tear gas until the National Guard sent sullen young men to sit in the street corners with only weapons and tired eyes. As I witnessed an empire in one of its worst years, I spent a lot of time with linden, acquainting myself with its powerful medicine. A handful of linden, half a scoop of tulsi and oats swirling in hot water until it was ready to be drunk. *Une poignée de tilleul, une demi-cuillère de tulsi et de l'avoine.* The teapot was always full. We all aged ten years that summer, as if the release of grief shocked all our bodies at once.

Every morning, I would listen to the French news to remind myself that there was a world outside of the few sidewalks of trauma I inhabited. Every morning, I would soothe myself with the language of the Empire that had raised me, more palatable because of its familiarity to my body. French news, linden tea. Every morning, I would try to remind myself of the stories of my people, and of everything that they held to be holy.

In the midst of the uprising and the pandemic, my phone rang with the news that Shyeed had died, his body punctured with enough bullets that he'd never see his son grow up. His life a currency of the Empire that extracted the holiness of his body. Twenty-three, and we had known each other for too long already, a relationship forced by courts and systems, a relationship that grew into the true love of lives intertwined anyways. I miss you Shyeed, even though I know that you come back every summer to visit, in the form of butterflies grazing linden flowers. I miss you Shyeed; I miss the version of you that I hadn't met yet, the one I could sense blooming at the edge of your lips. If only I could have protected your body in forests of freedom trees, away from the streets that would tear you apart. If only I could have carried your family to safety, your son, your wife, your favorite clothes, your bike. If only I could have taught you the shared ways of our ancestors, quietly hiding under the canopy. If only there were enough trees to uproot the horrors of living in the American city. If only there were enough linden trees to bring life back into your body. If only the American linden trees could write stories of freedom.

* * *

Linden has been holy for most of human history to every culture in which it has grown, used to heal the heart and release the tension in the body. Its tender smell opens the insides of us to possibilities not explored before. The bees know it, favoring the tree's delicate flowers to make equally delicate honey. But the tree itself is sweeter than honey, its leaves and flowers moistening the body when prepared in water.

In the herbalism I was taught, we know the linden to be a cooling plant that supports our nervous system, a plant that releases stress and that over time can bring down the blood pressure.

In the spiritual herbalism I favor, we know that the linden's essence can help us shift the pattern of holding the tension in the body and mind. A release of sorts. We practice taking gentle imprints of the flower by placing it delicately on top of a bowl of water. Mine, purchased in a thrift store, like every dish in my cabinets. Water, flowers set under the auspicious sun. Each movement an invitation and prayer for the plant to release her vibrations into the memory of the water. And when it's over and the water is charged with the personality of the plant, we'll conserve the energy with alcohol for the water to keep its magic for years to come.

When I teach others how to make flower essences, I teach them that it's a practice of relationship making, a way of moving away from consuming plants and getting to know them for their innate qualities, the joy and humor that make up their specific bodies. Sitting next to a bowl of water under the sun is a reminder that no matter what we believe we are, we are of the earth and that each element too has a personality akin to one of our friends. Some plants, I find arrogant, some I find to not be my taste, but together we build community regardless.

Taken orally over time a flower essence teaches our body to shift patterns. Slowly, gradually, away from the timelines of rushed capitalism. Linden releases blocks of energy stuck in the body and that summer I wanted to flood the streets of the Empire with the vibrations of the fragrant white flowers.

That summer of 2020, I worked with linden for the grief that took over my lungs, I couldn't breathe anything but the tar of death that surrounded us. Do you remember when we still counted the lives we had lost? When we marked the grim milestone? One-hundred thousand dead.

That summer when the grief was too much, I would leave the city gray for a few hours and bathe in the solid presence of trees. I would touch their bark like generations had done before me, letting the forest swallow me. I knew that the healing required of me could be found in their roots growing away from the concrete, building life at the center of this empire. An ancient being that had experienced plagues and the destruction of its life. Do you ever think about the loneliness of an urban tree? Alone surrounded by cement. Can they still communicate with their kin or are they forced to a life of isolation and despair? Can they hold on to the memory of the forest of their ancestors?

When I would drown in my own grief, when I could feel myself filled to the brim, I would go back to the lindens over and over. How much of their vibrations did I ingest before the energy shifted? I imagined my insides spilling on the asphalt of the city soaked in the blood of Shyeed. I hope you knew you were loved, even when your back was against the wall, sweet honey child. I hope you knew that the love we had for you would forever live in our lungs.

* * *

There isn't a French equivalent to the grief we use in English. We talk about *faire son deuil*, as in undertake our mourning. A task to accomplish. We talk about *chagrin, douleur*, to describe the pain of loss, words we use for other types of pain too. *Douleur*, as in the latin dolor derived from the Indo-European root of *delh*, to split. Just like the Sully trees, growing old in French villages, we find ourselves divided, our bodies contorting to accommodate this new reality, our minds cut from another version of ourselves who hadn't yet experienced the pain. Just like the Treblinka trees, we continue to grow on top of destruction, grimly expanding through the pain.

The feeling that has been filling my lungs steadily doesn't need words to be noticed. Bits of hope shrunk into nothingness, the darkness of loss. The feeling that has been filling my lungs steadily only needs to be noticed in the body, away from language, away from human constructions and ideas. Because there is no language I know that can make sense of this, the death, the Empire, the destruction of rituals and trees. There is no language that can make sense of the immensity of despair and violence that makes an American city. There are no words in French to describe the scale of destruction, no pun or poetic to tell you the immensity of energy stuck in the American body. Just the smell of lindens reminding us that another year has gone by, another year of sidewalks and trees growing older in a cloud of inescapable grief.

This Song is a Cover

HOW DO YOU START SOMETHING? YOU START IT.

I started writing to fill the gap left by the deep loss of six years of a relationship that had felt like rebuilding a family. It started with a promise made to myself to try something that felt uncomfortable, and to not let myself think about it too much. It was my attempt at building resilience in the face of what felt like rejection. My ultimate trigger.

As I wrote, I found space for the spirals of my own ruminations; a practice that allowed to make meaning of memories. When my friend Kelly tells me they're trying to write a book, I tell them that it's all about finding a practice that brings joy. What sustains you will grow.

How do you start something? You start it.

It was too cold to enjoy my walk, so I had to force myself to wander around the neighborhood. A humid and cold Sunday, the sun already low by mid-afternoon. To entertain myself, I stared at front yards, and imagined what the dead plants would look like by summer. I listened to songs that used to make up my internal landscape back in Paris, and I was suddenly transported to the feeling of paralysis that defined my twenties. As I spend too much time in my own head it has become a ritual to trigger myself by accident.

How do you start something? You start it.

It's 2008. Gilles and I had just come back from many months of traveling across the US with the excuse of filming a documentary about punk houses. The camera allowed us to insert ourselves in scenes that were adjacent to ours; we got to meet dozens of people who were friends of friends until we ran out of money and visas.

We flew back to France with a longer layover in Dublin, where we spent a few days. As I walked through the random bookstore in the center of town, I noticed my body panicking. I was going back to France, and I had no idea what life would be, who I wanted to be.

All I knew was that I was leaving behind a life that I wanted, a life of wandering and exploration, for the mundanity of a life I knew.

How do you start something? You start it.

In 2022, I listen to this BARR song that nobody listens to anymore and find myself paralyzed by multitudes, rendered immobile by imperfection. But these days, I have tools: I turn to the past and try to find answers, I remind myself of all the lessons I have learned over the years: so that I can stay grounded. I try to anchor into the present and remind myself that whatever I do becomes me, that whatever I practice becomes life. I have become better at acting even when I feel paralyzed, but the catastrophic trajectory of our species seems to be accelerating at a rate I can't keep up with.

How do you start something? You start it.

After my return to France that winter of 2008, I went back to waiting tables and bartending. A job I didn't like, that barely paid for my life in Paris. Every day, I would come home too exhausted to think about the future. The first electric bill that winter made me sob uncontrollably on the couch I shared with Gilles on the 7th floor of our Hausmannian building. That night I fell asleep on our mattress we had dragged from the street on the metro.

After a few months, we started hosting all the American punks who had extended generosity our way. It didn't matter that our tiny Parisian apartment couldn't hold all the bodies; we made it work.

How do you introduce something? You start it.

"I don't call you because I know you already have so much on your plate," Rainn tells me when I reach out. We met a few months ago when I facilitated an accountability process for their collective and we've stayed in touch since then.

"I didn't want to bother you with my problems, they're so small in comparison to everybody else's."

It's a refrain I have heard all week, as I call people to ask, "How are you?" I tell all the people I call that there is no hierarchy in suffering, and I recommend we knock other people's problems off the pedestal. Rainn finally admits, "My brother died last week." We process the loss.

I sit with that exchange for days, letting it swirl around my consciousness, wondering what it means to see death as not big enough to call. I understand the thought; I have had that thought before. I have that thought everyday as I read the headlines, and fail to read the full stories, too exhausted to absorb the competing immense tragedies that make up human life. How can there be room for our individual suffering? I make more phone calls and repeat my line about pedestals, knowing that the repetition isn't enough to change the pattern.

How do you start something? You start it.

I remember that year in Paris, I would listen to that BARR song again and again. I romanticize that time until I knock the memory off its pedestal and remember the crippling anxiety and loneliness that kept me indoors, paralyzed. I would come home exhausted from human interactions that took away my dignity. Over and over.

I left the bartending job in July, before starting school again that following fall. I had figured out a way to use my documentary after all; I was to enroll in a grad program in American visual culture where I would be writing about radical tradition and DIY.

Back then, writing meant sleepless nights and many days of crying afterwards. A daze of words covered in deep insecurity. *What do I have to add to the existing discourse?* I changed in the last decade; writing doesn't make me cry anymore. I have committed to failing again and again, sometimes publicly. The shame doesn't matter at all anymore: who has the time to ridicule me amid so many catastrophes?

How do you start something? You start it.

I have felt small this week; I have noticed my feelings being hurt more easily. I notice that sometimes the bonds that matter to me aren't reciprocal and I let the feeling wash over me. I spend more time than usual in rêverie, or if I'm being honest with you, I revert to my old self and let myself float outside of reality for stretches of time. It's easier to live in a daydream when the connections feel frayed. It's easier until you receive the call and hear the question being asked, "How are you?"

I wish I could tell you the question is enough to break the pattern, but it isn't. Not quite.

How do you start something? You rip something off.

I don't know how to tell you what shifted in me, once the distance felt big enough with my old self. I try, and fail, to convey the million small choices that add up to a different life.

In 2018, I bought a house. I bought it because I believed that we would live together when you came home from the walls that kidnapped you, Habib. I believed that if we purchased a solid structure, and decorated your room, you would come home faster. It was a practice in making miracles, to imagine you within our shared home, making tea and eating fresh fruit.

In our phone calls, we would fantasize about what you would wear once free. You wanted to regain your dignity by wearing slacks and ties and white shirts. And I wanted you to have a room and an office, because I believed that if we could build a container of safety, if you could have space away from an old life, you too could heal from the trauma.

In our phone calls, we would laugh about your love for Mimi the cat, and we would imagine what it would feel like to be together all the time. I wanted you home before she could die. Before you would die.

No more visiting rooms, where I would buy you the most expensive thing in the vending machine as a way of telling you how much you meant to me. No more holiday cards lost in the mail. No more count time, where you would have to unfurl your spine, and stand up with all the other men wearing jumpsuits, making sure that you stood tall to remind them the limits of their power. No more falling apart in the car, after our goodbyes, haunted by the image of your body lining the wall alongside other men as we stood with the other families leaving.

In that house, you and me and Johnny and Mimi, we could create a new life.

How do you start something? You rip something off.

When Habib stopped calling me after two years of daily phone calls, after six years of deep interdependence, I understood that the physical distance had created so many cracks in our foundation that it had all fallen apart. I understood that as freedom became more of a reality, he needed distance. I understood that he probably has an entirely different narrative, and that both our stories coexist within this universe as one braided thread.

After it all fell apart, I grieved, and I wallowed in the shame of not being what he needed me to be. I tried to hold on, but the connection had become so thin, the anger so big, that I was left with myself. Disconnected, again.

How do you start something? You start it.

When I feel desperate, I now know to put my fingers in the dirt of my garden. In the backyard of the house we won't be sharing, I grow flowers and trees and medicinal plants. This spring, I planted a cherry tree, next to the hawthorn and the elderberry bushes. I named it after a man who meant something to my neighbor, a man who died on the day I dug the hole to plant the tree.

On the days when I remember the paralysis of my youth, on the days when I am so nostalgic, I feel like a caricature of myself, I pull out every seedling that isn't welcome, I notice the worms and the pill bugs, I transplant what needs more room to grow. I move away from saying I garden, because the word doesn't paint the spiritual picture of this practice.

It is a practice of miracle making, the ritual of believing that with time and water and attention, seeds transform into healing. It is a practice of cellular reorientation, that reconnects my nervous system to an ecosystem capitalism keeps me mostly disconnected from.

In the kitchen, the grow lights make everything look pink and blue. *Bisexual lighting*, they call it. Row after row of thyme and chamomile seedlings to replace the weeds, tulsi, tomatoes from saved seeds. Every container reminds me that it all starts with soil and a seed and the trust that a speck will unfurl into leaves.

How do you start something? You rip something off.

On a Saturday morning, after the last frost has passed, I walk around the neighborhood with my friend Mina. It's a habit we developed months ago, a weekly ritual of coffee and sometimes croissants, where we catch up. "How are you?" She's drowning in grief, and I sometimes am too.

We walk past a once-punk house now being sold for close to a million dollars, sporting one of those realtor signs that tells me my neighborhood has shifted even quicker than expected, a constant anxiety familiar to anybody living in an American city. The former tenants have piled up the remains of the house in cardboard boxes labeled "FREE" and Mina and I rummage. We find shirts and tote bags to put them in, she finds copies of Doris zines, wondering out loud which of the former roommates left them behind. Remnants of a time that maybe has passed. I have rummaged through hundreds of free piles all over this country; sometimes it feels like I'm getting too old for the free piles, sometimes it feels like I am rummaging through my own youth.

As I look through the CDs, I find a copy of *Beyond the Reinforced Jewel*, BARR's 2005 record that starts with this song. *A cover, it's really begun already.*

I see this CD, on the porch of this defunct punk house as a sign of changing eras, a portal to times past. A neglected copy of this song that means so much to me seventeen years later, discarded on a stoop. I think about the ex-lover who introduced me to BARR back in the Bay Area; I think about how we don't talk anymore, too much time has passed. Hard to not see a metaphor there. I pick it up and bring it home, even though I don't own a CD player anymore.

How do you start something? You start it.

Inside my own mind, I lament the limitations of the English language, even though it is the language I choose when I write. I try to think about clever ways to tell the story of redemption that comes from putting your fingers in soil.

I talk about it with friends who have also found their trajectories shifted by their practice of land tending and we complain about all the different ways we fail at explaining reciprocity. In a world of consumption, how do you explain holy transmutation?

I play with the sentence structure and try to imagine more scenes to express the vastness of meaning behind the simple practice of putting your fingers in the soil. The safety, the care. They say the smell of soil releases endorphins. That it reminds the brain of the connection to our caregivers. I stand in the yard and make mental notes of the wind, that ray of sun, the different shades of green, the bee on the monarda, the hops that grow so fast you can see it with your own eyes on a summer day. But I fail to convey the depth of the experience.

With my inability to fully convey this miracle comes the realization that my failure is rooted in the sacredness of the practice. Because holiness is what makes a place, a person, an idea more beautiful than the sum of its parts. Impossible to document in its fullness. And sometimes, the failure is a reminder of the miracle. Sometimes, the failure contains a story of times passed, millions of changes, each of them imperceptible. Together, though, they create change of such magnitude that it hits us with the force of every moment, person, place we have mourned and will mourn until we are ourselves the object of mourning for others.

And with that realization comes the peace of knowing that in this moment of unfolding catastrophe, I am human after all. Simply trying to tell a story of beginnings, ends, and in-betweens.

How do you start something? You rip something off.

Linden Tea Recipe

1. Wait until July, when the temperatures stop cooling at night. Notice the ways your body remembers the anniversary of your grief.

2. Ask them to drive you to the large linden tree in the Centennial Park because you still haven't learned how to operate a car. Bring a book, a blanket. You two will enjoy its shade as you read with your bodies intertwined.

3. Put your book down while they read. Realize you haven't brought a paper bag. Use the torn up one your chalupa came in. Spots of grease. Walk to the tree and thank her for her existence.

4. Hold the trunk, caress the bark, feel the energy of your kin. Admire the darkness of the linden tree leaves.

5. Gently pick flowers off the branches. Marvel at their fruity smell. Don't be greedy, the hole in your bag prevents you from taking too much. Worry about other people seeing you harvest the leaves and telling you you're not allowed.

6. Place the flowers on the drying rack Johnny built for your birthday. Spread them into a thin layer.

7. Transfer the dry flowers in a container. Marvel at the bounty of the Earth, the fleeting moment of fragrant flowers.

8. Grab a handful of flowers, enough to drown the breaking of your heart and place in a cup. Pour hot water and cover the cup. Wait. Wait.

9. Strain the flowers and thank them for their medicine. Release them to the ancestors.

10. Drink your tea, quietly, breathing deeper and deeper with every sip.

Monster

"**A**MERICANS ARE STUPID," I KEEP REPEATING TO VARI-
ous cab drivers, this time to Manuel who's driving
me from the small Oaxaca airport to the residency
where I'll be spending the next two weeks. It's my first time outside of
the American Empire in three years; I took two flights to get here, one
from an American city to another American city, another one from an
American city to the Mexican mountains, crossing the border with my
French passport. I am here to study poleo, a plant I was introduced
to by a Zapotec woman six years ago and that I have, until now, understood to be an ancestral plant of mine. I am coming to Oaxaca to
edit an essay about colonialism and my place in the world, that has
been sitting in my drafts for many months, unfinished without the
reconnection to the original plant.

"Americans are stupid," I say to cab drivers, even though I have the
immense privilege of a green card sitting comfortably in my pocket
next to my money and credit cards. Manuel tells me about his family
members who moved to Corpus Christi twenty years ago; their lack
of papers prevents them from coming back to Oaxaca to visit and he
hasn't seen them since. Their children, born in the United States, come

to visit sometimes, but they have never known anything else about Mexico. They are a little lost in the land of their ancestors.

In DC, a few months ago, Ahmed told me he drives Uber night and day to save enough money to send to his village, and how for the first time in years he was able to visit his homeland of Ethiopia. He does not understand why American society is centered around loneliness instead of community and can't wait to leave.

In Philly, where I live, Fasim yells "Fuck the French, they're all thieves. They took everything from our people." Our people, meaning his country of Sudan, and my ancestral Morocco. "But, habibti, you need to learn Arabic," he adds as he rushes through red lights. Fasim is grateful for the money he makes here, but can't fathom bringing his children to this country. He can't allow them to be exposed to the violence that rhythms our streets.

Those exchanges always end with the cab drivers asking, expectantly: "And what about your family? Are they still in France? Are they still in Morocco?" and I diplomatically tell them that there is no family anymore, because it's easier than to explain violence, abuse and disconnection.

When I tell cab drivers "Americans are stupid," I mean to say that America lured me with the promises of endless freedom away from the life I had in France. And that some of that freedom did materialize for me but somewhere along the way, I lost too many parts of myself. That I had dreamt about this move for years before it happened, and that now I wonder why. What I really mean to say when I say "Americans are stupid," is that America swallowed me and that I can't recognize myself in the shadow of this Empire.

* * *

This was supposed to be a story about how a trip to a Zapotec village reconnected me with an ancestral plant relative of mine. Instead, it became a story of translations and monsters.

* * *

In my native French and Hebrew, language is gendered, meaning that nouns and pronouns, assigned to objects and beings, carry the mark of the masculine and feminine. Often, the rules of such gendering confuses non-native speakers, who fail to understand how to know which binary to assign. In French the cathedral is feminine, the convent isn't. An animal is masculine whereas a plant isn't. It's a taxonomy that shapes the world of those who speak the language, a sort of certainty that lives in the body.

My mother, who learned French after her migration, would often mix up masculines and feminines, to our dismay. I was embarrassed at her mistakes, I could not understand how her eyes viewed the world. I didn't understand why she could never assign the right gender to what was around her, not even to me, her child.

* * *

Everybody knows I'm a motherfuckin' monster.

* * *

Six years ago, I traveled to Mexico for the first time, right after the American elections that shook us all, in the midst of my own green card process. I had always dreamed of traveling to Mexico, but I can't quite remember what prompted this specific trip. A week in Mexico City, another in Oaxaca with some smaller cities in between. Maybe it was that I was finally able to leave the confines of the United States borders, and maybe I had grown timid and too scared to stray too far from them.

I had only started to work a year before, a part-time position teaching English to adult immigrants. Together, we practiced the different sounds an American existence requires. We explored all the ways the American mind felt different to us, illogical, naive. We lamented the ways everything was about money in this country. Yet, we had all made the choice. Maybe that's why I went to Mexico, to hear the Spanish that I had grown fond of.

On that first trip to Oaxaca, I got sick. The type of sick that happens in foreign countries, where time stands still as your body purges itself. An inadequately washed vegetable, bad water, an ice cube disturbing the digestive system. It always feels like the world ends in those moments, but in that occurrence, the timing was indeed inconvenient. Johnny and I had planned and paid for a hike in the Pueblos Mancomunados, and I needed my body to recover quickly to withstand the long walks through cloud forests and fields.

It was supposed to be one of the highlights of this trip, three days in the Sierra Norte mountains, walking between remote villages, while supporting a tourism cooperative of indigenous Zapotec communities. It was an attempt at finding right relationship in the act of being a tourist, supporting indigenous sovereignty, while walking off the proverbial beaten path.

Despite my weakened system, we decided to go through with the hike and left Oaxaca before the sun rose, to meet our guide in the small village of Cuajimoloyas, a couple of hours north of the city. While waiting for our hike to start, as it was still early in the day, we stopped at the village's comedor, for breakfast. Because of my very limited Spanish and inability to eat solid food, I signaled to the cook that I could use a cup of tea. Mentha perhaps. Manzanilla. She offered me poleo rubbing her stomach to let me know it would support my digestive system. I didn't know what poleo was, but I instantly liked its pungent flavor, its pepperiness similar to mountain mint in its strength. With that first cup, I noticed my belly relaxing with contentment, settling. I felt better, happy, on top of this mountain, waiting for my world to open up.

From this first trip to Oaxaca, I came back to the United States with a small pouch of poleo I bought from the mercado 20 de noviembre. I felt a connection to the plant that I couldn't quite explain and wanted to build a deeper bond. Extensive internet searches taught me that poleo was pennyroyal (*mentha pulegium*) and I believed it because that's what you're supposed to do. I combed through articles about Mexican poleo tea and that same week I bought a bag of pennyroyal from an herbal store in Philadelphia, amazed at the coincidence, trying to reverently build relationship with this mystical plant I had met on top of a Zapotec mountain.

In my research, I learned that pennyroyal is endemic to the Mediterranean basin and North Africa, and that meant I had met an ancestor of mine on top of that mountain. As if the plant had wanted to find me.

On the Internet, I found narratives of pennyroyal being introduced to Mesoamerica by its colonizers, Arabs coming within the destruction of the Spaniard conquest. I do not know if there is any truth to this story but when I read it, I found solace in the original sins of crossing worlds, familiar in their brutality.

* * *

I have always known I wasn't a girl, and assumed that my parents did too, because of their constant policing of my gender. Early on, I believed that my existence at the edges of the gendered binaries was a sign of monstrousness. Without the words to express those differences, I looked for texts to tell me who I was, I read about hermaphrodites and autogynephilia. I wondered if I was a boy, or if I was just a freak, bound to never be loved. It was the nineties in France, there wasn't much I could find and I knew I was a unicorn of a child but I worried I was a chimera. Puberty felt like a cruel joke, shifting my flat chest into growing breasts, distorting my hips and rearranging my features.

As a teen, I would dream terrifying night visions of being found out, of people paying attention to my body and discovering it wasn't what it should look like. As if my transness could be read in the body that everybody else understood as the body of a girl. As if there was something shameful in my shape. But the shame, the shame suffocated me, leaving no room for breath.

For the first part of my twenties, I decided to try hard to be a girl, wearing makeup, flats and dresses, plucking and waxing, convincing myself that this was what I longed for. An exercise of drag, a desperate attempt at translating what was wanted of me. I never felt like I could measure up to the intense regimens required by French femininity, I felt trapped. "Excellente présentation" required in job listings. Not a day without foundation, mascara. Learning to shrink the body by starving it, in order to be a girl. Straightened hair and plucked eyebrows. And still there was something constantly eluding me, something I couldn't put my finger, something out of my reach.

In those years, during my visits to the US, chasing bands whose music I admired, I would marvel at the punk girls with leg hair growing wild, mustaches blooming even as I had been trying to eliminate mine since I was ten. They seemed to find power in letting their bodies unfurl, otherworldly creatures I wished to emulate. They seemed to relish the ambiguity I had tried to kill within me.

When English became my primary language, after I had moved for good, something shifted in me as if the language allowed for more room for my ideas of myself to grow. In English, I could potentially let go of the idea of being a boy or a girl altogether; I could stay in the third place I had always occupied, and have the language to describe it.

Maybe this newfound freedom was the result of the shift in language. Maybe it was the realization that in this process of migration, I had lost my capacity to be fully human again, having left my shadow somewhere above an ocean.

* * *

When I decided to stay in the United States and get a green card, I had already lived in many countries, zigzagging through various land masses in my quest for a home.

While deeply rooted in the privilege of my citizenship and circumstances, the immigration process was traumatic. After a couple years of roaming together around different continents, Johnny and I got married, something we had tried to avoid for the length of our relationship that started only three months before my American visa expired and I had to leave the country. Our love felt like a finding of home, a settling into certitudes that I was scared of shifting by making it more legible to the world.

I knew that in the process of documenting ourselves for the state, in the act of asking agents of a government to recognize us, we would break some of our magic, lose some of us. I worried that in the definition, we would try to masquerade a love that wasn't ours to perform.

Yet, on a summer day, we signed papers required of us, before building files of every letter, picture, stories that proved us, I got vaccinations shots, we asked people who knew us to confirm that we were indeed, in love, and sent those forms to the immigration office and waited.

In that long process, for over a year, I was not allowed to cross the border or work, for years after I had to build a life quickly, frenetically to catch up on all the time I had lost living other lives.

The stories we built for me to receive the small plastic card validating my life in this country started to change me. I noticed myself shrinking, dimming and hardening, necessary survival strategies to survive the American Empire. I adapted to the circumstances of this new life. I noticed that most people around me, people dedicating their life to the dismantling of American cruelty, didn't notice the ways their minds were altered by the reality of living on this land. Inside the crevice of my chest, above my head I went.

In those first years living in the United States as a permanent resident, I practiced leaving my French vowels and consonants behind. I morphed my mouth to shape itself around an imaginary hot potato, to soften the edges of my "r" and "I". I dropped the diphthongs that made my tongue tingle with the certitude of home. I practiced pronouncing "h" like the Americans do and I mimicked the words I heard people around me say. Through language I performed new skins. I wanted to blend in, belong to this place. I wanted desperately to have a place to call home again, even if it meant shedding parts of what home meant to me. In that process of embodying a new language, I started losing my French, one word at a time.

Memories of past life, requiring me to examine them in the tongue of my birth. Who was I without the sounds of my former home?

In my then-apartment in Philadelphia, as I tried to piece together a life, building a relationship with plants allowed me to connect to a sense of self, of a bigger world out there. After that first bag of poleo, I bought more. Lemon balm, tulsi, mints. Each plant constructing a story about hope, possibility, futures. I held on to the mythology of poleo because it allowed me to make sense of a fragmented self crossing borders, shaped by colonial lands and words. It was just a fantasy.

* * *

When I turned eight or nine, my parents built the attic into an expansion of our apartment. I asked for my room to be painted green, my favorite color then. I tried not to cry as I entered it first, walls painted shades of light pink and suffocating ruby carpet. An injunction.

* * *

In Mexico, I notice my mouth freezing, fumbling over Spanish words I know. I understand the language, and yet my body is refusing to let me communicate in it. I listen to long conversations spoken by rapid tongues and make sense of meanings easily, but when it is time for me to open my mouth and speak, I am paralyzed. The words stored within me refuse to spill out, stuck in the body. As if my lips, palate and teeth were denying me another transformation, as if I was refusing to adopt yet another new way of understanding the world. I keep wondering who I could be in Spanish, in this new shape of my mouth, what shames and stories I would shed.

* * *

After my move to America I stopped wearing dresses altogether, and let go of the hair removal routine that had become part of my life. I dressed like I did in my childhood, striped shirts, overalls, jeans, hoodies. I covered my body with art: a woman with a mustache, an androgynous creature, birds, plants, prayers. I sought and met people who, like me, tried to embody their wildest selves. Divine minds whose internal understanding of themselves didn't match the ways the world saw them or wanted them to be seen.

In my early thirties, after years of pondering, I started asking others to use the pronoun "they" to describe me. When their mouths would pronounce this simple syllable, I would feel delight, noticing the parts of me that softened in contentment, the parts of me that moved closer to the light.

In this act of translating myself to others, I would even believe that my body held beauty and could be desired for what it truly was rather than what I was forcing it to become.

* * *

When I come back to Oaxaca, in the last days of 2022, I arrive dazed at 2:00PM to a beautiful house organized around a courtyard. My room is on the roof that offers sweeping views of the Sierras that surround the city. I left my home of Philadelphia at 4:00AM, hoping to find some new stories of myself in another country. It has always worked for me.

I immediately set out to find poleo in the market, and do so with incredible ease at a small stand that showcases a variety of dried herbs. In the mercado, women from the nearby villages sell it in bundles, alongside chamomile, marigold, and pericón. I hold this moment with anticipation, I imagine myself holding this plant I have grown to love, I imagine myself holding a story I have made up in my mind. Something about kinship to the Earth regardless of our location.

Thirty-five pesos later, I hold a bundle of herbs tied to each other with dried grass. But the poleo I am holding is not the pennyroyal I have planted in my garden, grown amongst ancestral rue, wormwood and mint. It is a different plant altogether, long stalks ending with a beautiful ruby flower that looks nothing like the short stalks covered in tufts of purple that I have grown to love. The story I had held on to for six years, created by the imperfection of translation and my yearning for belonging crashes down in that moment of a single meaningless transaction.

* * *

I have been agonizing over the decision to get top surgery for years. My breasts have grown larger with age and I know that there would be some joy in removing them, a feeling of euphoria that often eludes me, a turning back of the clock to a childhood sense of freedom. A sense of home within my body, of expansion of its borders. There's a heightened risk of cancer that would disappear too.

But I feel protective of my nipples. It's silly, but I do not want them to go or change. I do not know if I am willing to exchange the uncomfortable mounds of flesh for scars. I do not want my monstrosity to be displayed for all to see.

I give myself more time to think about it, and wince at the discomfort of my gender being misunderstood. I still look like a woman. I am aware that the body I want to have only exists in my head, a story I concocted many decades ago. A fantasy easier to embody within the confines of my mind. Can it be enough to name my differences if they're only visible to me? Is it enough for me to use new words if the shape that speaks them hasn't changed? In my body, the fear of the many borders I will still need to transgress in this lifetime.

* * *

In his plant taxonomy published in 1789, on the eve of the French revolution, under the title of *Genera Plantarum*, French botanist Jussieu categorized some twenty thousand plants based on their various attributes: shape of leaves and stalks, roots, reproductive tendencies. This document would lay the foundation of botany as we know it today, and determine the various families, genus and varieties of plants around the world, assigning them Latin names so that they can be understood in various linguistic contexts.

At the ethnobotanical garden of Oaxaca, the guide tells our group that there aren't any Latin words for a variety of plants used in indigenous communities. Only words in Mixtec or Zapotec because the plants do not exist anywhere else.

This isn't the case for poleo. Poleo from the Oaxaca region is known in latin as *Clinopodium Macrostemum*, a member of the *Lamiaceae* families, the family that encompasses all mints, sages, basils. In other regions of Mexico, poleo means *mentha pulegium*, known in English as pennyroyal, in French as menthe pouliot, in Moroccan Arabic as fliou. In other places in Mexico, poleo means *Hedeoma Drummondii*, a plant I don't know anything about. All three of them can be poleo, depending on the mouth that speaks their name into existence. All three plants are part of the Lamiacae family.

Lamiaceae are defined by their characteristic 4-sided stems and opposite leaves, as well as their aromatic properties thanks to volatile oils that they contain. A rubbing of a Lamiaceae plant will produce a fragrant aroma, that for most of them holds a calming effect. Pennyroyal and Oaxacan poleo produce similar scents, overlapping in their properties of soothing both the thoughts and the body.

When Jussieu named the plants Lamiaceae, he derived their name from the Latin Lamia, which describes a blood sucking witch, an antique daemon of Greek mythologies.

Different narrators describe Lamia as either Poseidon's daughter, the daughter of the King of Egypt or the Queen of Libya. Regardless of her pedigree, they all agree that her beauty attracted the attention of Zeus who seduced her and made her his mistress. The infidelity enraged his wife Hera, who decided to punish his lover. Hera's curse instantly killed Lamia's children, also hexing any new children she would give birth to.

Disfigured and overwhelmed by the grief of such immense loss, Lamia became an ogress, roaming the world to steal newborns she would devour in the cave that had become her lair. Her story became a cautionary tale, told from generation to generation, sometimes as half-human half-serpent to misbehaving children.

In the shape of the Lamiaceae flowers, Jussieu saw the hungry lips of a monstrous and ravenous woman. I look at the poleo, the Oaxacan poleo, the *Climapodium Macrostemum* and in its ruby red flower I see a bird in flight.

* * *

On my last visit to Paris, a few years ago, I meet an old friend at a café and he tells me that I now speak my native French with an American accent. My palate deformed by my dreams of new worlds, my former self lost in the translation of myself. I don't correct him when he uses "elle" to describe me. Even after I told him the story of my body. Four letters reminding me, I am invisible, lost between worlds, in exile from myself.

* * *

In Spanish, poleo is also known as herba del borracho: herb of the drunk, used after nights of partying to relieve the body of hangovers. In the Oaxaca region, poleo is also used to flavor food, support the unsettled stomach, relieve migraines and relax the body. A gentle plant that grows abundantly on the slopes of Mexican mountains, long stalks, oblong leaves, bright red flowers. She looks nothing like my ancestral plant, the poleo I thought she was for so long, the menthe pouliot and fliou of my people, the pennyroyal of American minds.

In her native lands of North Africa, Europe and the Middle East, pennyroyal grows as a wild weed, nurtured by wet patches and incessant sun. Her body stays close to the ground before growing shoots that flower with delicate tufts of pink and purple.

She was beloved by the Romans, who added her to wines and foods for flavoring. In his Natural History, Pliny the Elder described that: "Pennyroyal partakes with mint, in a very considerable degree, the property of restoring consciousness in fainting fits; slips of both plants being kept for the purpose in glass bottles filled with vinegar. It is for this reason that Varro has declared that a wreath of pennyroyal is more worthy to grace our chambers than a chaplet of roses: indeed, it is said that, placed upon the head, it materially alleviates headache."

Nowadays, pennyroyal is more famous for its abortifacient property, her capacity of removing from the body foreign masses that are not wanted. A power that shifted humans' relationship to the plant; over the centuries she has become less used, feared by some, revered by others.

* * *

So I, I am headed home.

* * *

In my room on the roof of the residency house, I make myself poleo tea in the morning to remember the person I was the first time the warm liquid touched my lips. Small, scared, adrift.

In the morning shade, I crush dried leaves in the palm of my hand and smell the fragrant oils, appreciating the plant for who she is. In the act of witnessing her, I practice letting go of the stories I had created about her and let myself approach her without the barrier of language and translation.

I have decided to refrain from extensive searches in books and archives; I realize I want to know the plant outside of the limitations of language.

Just me, a handful of leaves, and hot water, two curious creatures entering a new relationship, away from shame, fantasies and thesauri, a relationship of truths and bodies. I enjoy poleo, whoever she is. I want to savor her flavor, learn how ingesting her affects me. I am trying to excavate facts and sensations rather than myths and stories.

And I wonder what words she would use to describe me, if she could indeed use the flowers of her ravenous lips to speak. I wonder what version of me she can sense or if she is able to hold them all within her stalk, leaves and beak. And I wonder, if it would even matter now that I am ready to learn this new shared language, see what becomes of me, and reinvent shared territories.

To Walter

This seeking for my home…was my affliction…Where is—my home? I ask and seek and have sought for it; I have not found it"

—Nietzsche, Also sprache Zarathustra
as quoted in *The Arcades Project* by Walter Benjamin, pg. 20

THE FINAL TEAR WITH MY MOTHER STARTS WITH MY "FLÂNE" tattoo, the first tattoo that I give myself, in the first days of August 2012, at the age of twenty-seven, after deciding I would never live in France again. There is something bittersweet about it; there is something thrilling about it. I am giving up the country of my youth to stay in a Midwestern college town that makes me feel a foreignness new to my body; I am continuing a lineage of migration spanning generations; I am giving up my relationship to family to build myself anew. In the short few months of the summer, I will end a long term relationship, drop out of grad school and create walls of safety between me and my family. Sitting on the floor of the apartment I am subletting from an Ann Arbor student eager to break her lease, I wrap thread around a sewing needle and pen, dip them into ink, and gently poke my thigh. In that moment I force myself towards the decision to break the ties, to let it all go. Every dot on my skin another step towards the embodiment of myself. Flâne, as the injunction, the imperative tense, and the invitation to walk (away). A cord-cutting ritual.

* * *

From the earliest of ages, I remember myself being fascinated by cities and the freedom that they offered. When other children spent their time playing sports and socializing with each other, my sibling and I, punished into staying home, would look out our window in Mulhouse, gawk at the passersby enjoying a stroll and popping in and out of the stores of our street, and describe to each other what we saw. We lived at the center of town, on a pedestrian street, above a jewelry store that would become a tobacco shop in my teens, across from a carpet store that would become a beer hall. Mulhouse was small, suffocating, like the apartment I was being raised in. I lived a small life, contained by the perimeter of the city's layout.

I dreamed of documenting every face I saw on the street, I fantasized of documenting every building I encountered. I imagined myself running away. Elbows on the window ledge, we would pay attention to the ways adults moved their bodies and dressed themselves; we would invent stories to explain the behaviors and habits of the people we saw. The woman, distraught, pushing a stroller, the pouting child walking a few meters behind their parents, the laughing couple sitting at the café. Who were they? What did their lives look like away from this street?

When asked who I wanted to be when I grew up, all I wanted was an apartment in a big city, where I could disappear.

* * *

In 2022, a decade after that summer day in Ann Arbor, as my life has shifted in ways I would never have imagined back then, this crooked tattoo inspired by Walter Benjamin and his ruminations about city life and modernity is still one of the Frenchest thing about me, second only to the one on my leg of the writer Colette wearing a suit and smoking a cigarette. The block letters orient towards my eye, so that every time I look at my legs, my only mode of transportation, I get to remember that they are my way towards the life I want, an ode to impermanence and urban leisure. An anchor to a different time in my life. My accent has faded over the years, and sometimes I read the letters on my leg as if they were written in English. Flâne. A world-making ritual. A prayer for worlds to unfold.

I often think about that summer of 2012, the loneliness and mania that engulfed me then. I was spiraling, falling in love with everybody around me, distracting myself from the reality that I was changing lives, destroying paths to simple returns. I often wonder what portals this simple tattoo, five letters on my thigh, opened for me. What would have happened if I hadn't done that, if I hadn't let myself free fall the way I did. Who would I be?

* * *

"Ima I'm home," I announce as I enter the bedroom. It is a Friday afternoon sometimes in early 2004. I am nineteen, and I am coming home to Mulhouse for the weekend. My fully dressed mother is laying in her bed watching TV under the blankets, blinds closed in the middle of the day, a familiar sight. The air is heavy with the scent of her body. She smiles at me, her body lighting up at the reunion, until her eyes meet the shine of the piece of metal embedded in my left cheekbone. It is a new adornment acquired during a moment of bravery in a small shop located in the middle of les Halles, in the center of Paris where I am going to college. In the blink of a moment, her face falls, her eyes harden as she turns away from me and resumes her study of the movement on the screen. "Ima, I'm home," I repeat, my voice softer, unsure, as I watch her refuse to meet my eye. The joy of my return is over, we will both drown in her silence. Two days later, without another word, I board the train that will bring me back to my apartment in Paris.

* * *

You do not finish your French education without reading his words. Walter Benjamin. I remember reading his work about art and its aura in my late teens and how reading him expanded my understanding of the world. It was in an art history class, sometime in 2003, in a school where I was dedicating myself to the study of books. Selling them, publishing them, organizing them in the library. A slim volume I bought in a Parisian FNAC that shocked me with the simplicity of its prose and the complexity of its ideas. Of course, art has an aura, of course it means something else to interact with it without intermediary, of course there is sacredness in the experience. We shared a love for Baudelaire and the labyrinth of Parisian narrow streets. I loved him instantly, this Jewish German man with glasses similar to the ones I was still wearing back then. Walter and I shared an understanding of what sacredness means; I think he would agree on what I consider holy. Over the years, I would continue developing my relationship to his work and everybody who placed themselves in its lineage; I spent a lot of my time trying to make sense of the world we lived in and trying to see the way capitalism had eroded life. My love of books and art and cities that will eventually lead me to that apartment in an American college town for a year-long fellowship in August of 2011.

* * *

"We are bored when we don't know what we are waiting for. That we do know, or think we know, is nearly always the expression of our superficiality or inattention. Boredom is the threshold to great deeds …Now, it would be important to know: What is the dialectical antithesis to boredom?" —Walter, pg. 105

* * *

On a humid day of August 2011, my partner Gilles and I wheel our overstuffed suitcases from the Megabus station at the edge of town to the apartment we will move into, found by a friend who magically lived in Ann Arbor already. Above our hoarding landlady, only a few blocks from the campus that will become my home.

I have given up on my dreams of selling books by then. Instead, I am focusing on my ideas, writing a dissertation that would make me Dr. Keim. In Ann Arbor, my fellowship requires me to teach French to overachieving students, in exchange for the access to the books of an American University. I am writing an expansion of my master's thesis, a cultural history of the Mission District of San Francisco. I am writing about the making of a city's visual culture and the ways art preceded and accelerated its gentrification. I read about social movements, queer art and punk history; I examine high definition pictures of murals and old store signs; I scan listing of shows in video stores and warehouses. I have proposed to my committee an examination of the layers of one small section of the city and try to do justice to the The Clarion Alley murals, the Galeria de la Raza, the Black Panther Party, the Epicenter,

Los Siete de La Raza, 924 Gilman, Maximum Rock'n'roll and Counter-pulse. I want to show how the commodification of radical ideals created a terrain for their destruction.

Gilles doesn't work, waiting for his own fellowship in Johannesburg to start the following winter. We have made plans: at the end of my time in the Midwest, I will fly and meet him there, the two of us working towards PhDs. But after he leaves, the doubt spreads: is this the life I want? What if I gave myself the room to explore lives I had never imagined before? Who am I to write about stories that aren't mine to tell? Do I want to live a life approved by my parents?

As the end of my time in Ann Arbor nears, I learn that the French department needs a lecturer for the Spring and Summer semester and they offer me to stay as a full-time lecturer. I make a series of rash decisions, quit my PhD and relationship to focus my attention on building a new life. For years after I will dwell on the shame of those decisions, the ties cut with the frenzy of uncertainty.

The vastness of the ocean that separates me from my former life, relationship, and rhythm gives me permission to dream of new paths. I imagine myself teaching and preparing myself to apply to an American PhD program, where I could continue to study cities. Or I could leave the Midwest and move to Mexico City, where I could learn Spanish. Or I could teach French anywhere, untied to anybody or anything, only guided by the infinite streets of desire.

* * *

The Arcades Project is a sprawling document, scribbled on pieces of paper, left under the care of surrealist writer and philosopher George Bataille in 1940, when Benjamin had to flee Paris because of the Nazi invasion. Bataille, then a librarian at the Bibliothèque Nationale de France hid the documents that would be retrieved after the war and meticulously put together by Theodor Adorno and other friends. It is an intriguing project; Benjamin in his massive accumulation of fragments tries to build the city under the layers of capitalism that have both built and disrupted its aura. He creates a cast of tropes and images: the flâneur, the gambler, the collector, as well as sets of urban images in the arcades, railroads and omnibus. It is hard to convey the weight of seemingly endless quotes, references and thought spirals. Each fragment is marked with a section letter and number, creating connections with other fragments. It is a masterpiece and a ruin all at once.

* * *

In the early summer of 2012, after dropping out of grad school, I go back to France one last time and within minutes of sitting in my childhood apartment, I fall apart, crying at the reality I am facing. My parents are yelling about something or other, guilting me into crossing a boundary I have just enunciated. There is nothing left for me to do here, no relationship to hold onto. The end of the visit is a silent one, but this time, in my suitcase, I have packed my birth certificate, my school records and small mementos of the life I am leaving. I say goodbye to my books, the creak of the stairs, the smoothness of the tile in the hallway, the salmon pink of the restaurant across the street, the oak in the park I played in every day as a child, the distinctive smell of the train station hall. I say goodbye to my mother, knowing this is the last time we will embrace.

* * *

Some might think that being a flâneur is a privileged existence. Dandies walking the streets in their best attire, Baudelaire spending his inheritance on clothes, books and alcohol, the leisure of strolling the Parisian arcades, wasting a time that could otherwise be commodified. But Walter argued that slowing down to embrace the street of the city disrupts the forces of capitalism, that those of us who practice the sacred art of walking the streets and letting their life take over, are engaging in a radical practice. In his personal lifetime, the practice of making sense of urban life repeatedly brought him to the brink of bankruptcy. In 1932, as the Nazis rose to power, he left Germany, trying to find homes in Ibiza, Marseille, Denmark and Paris. In each place, he relied on the generosity and safety provided by friends. The movement around countries became a necessity for his survival, even if it meant renouncing other life joys. Many times, Walter considered death as the only step, until he found a way to his next stop.

For me, being a flâneur has grown from a desperate need for wandering that has rearranged my entire existence. Multiple jobs at once, sharing beds with unsafe people, and using the advantages granted by a free French education. A life of taking opportunities for movement and letting go of any semblance of stability. Compromised standards of excellence, sparse possessions, life lived out of backpacks, money stretched to impossible miracles for the joy of exploring new cities at the slow pace of my steps. None of it quite erasing the scarcities of my childhood. Some might say, a privileged existence nonetheless.

* * *

I can still walk the streets of my Mulhouse in my head, I can zoom in and out and see every single store and sidewalk of my hometown. I haven't set foot there in a decade now, and yet, I see it clearly. A left from our building and I pass the coffee shop, the bakery, the stamps store, a right at the Alsatian restaurant and I am in the alleyway that brings me to the park. Go around it, past the small museum, and another left and here's the theater, the hotel we could never afford. What I see of my former home are the stores and institutions that made our town, each one attached to stories and feelings and meaning. A place I dreamed of leaving for as long as I remember, forever etched into my brain.

Over the years, after I did indeed run away, I developed more maps of the mind: in Paris, San Francisco, New York and Mexico City and Kathmandu, DC, Hanoi and Kuala Lumpur, Bombay, Budapest, Hong Kong and Berlin, Amsterdam, Barcelona and Varanasi, Bangkok, Phnom Penh and Prague. Each city became the terrain of my imagination, creating room for possibilities and reinvention, putting more distance between the child staring out the window and the life they dreamed of and could finally actualize as an adult.

* * *

"The street conducts the flâneur into a vanished time. For him, every street is precipitous. It leads downward— if not to the mythical Mothers, then into a past that can be all the more spellbinding because it is not his own, not private. Nevertheless, it always remains the time of a childhood. But why that of the life he has lived? In the asphalt over which he passes, his steps awaken a surprising resonance. The gaslight that steams down on the paving stones throws an equivocal light on this double ground." —Walter, pg. 416

* * *

That late summer in Ann Arbor my return from France sees me fall apart at the seams. That summer, I ward off the bubbling grief by losing myself in books, mountains of them littering the floor of my apartment, taking unrelated notes on scraps of paper until I can't follow the thread of my own brain anymore.

In the pages of my notebook of that summer, I find remnants of ideas:

A. " Sight Sacralization—5 phases"
1. Naming
2. Framing
3. Enshrinement
4. Mechanical reproduction
5. Social reproduction—Dean Mac Connell—The tourist, A New Theory of the Leisure Class, 1976

B. "Historical reality, theatrical reality of conflict and power."

C. *Can you be a flâneur in SF?* Scribbled next to a quote from James Brook, "The images are empty of imagination and desire: without its memories, the city is a dead place and this has something to do with unhappiness and memory."

In the corner of that page I wrote "We all sing a different song," upside down in purple ink.

D. " Exil= réinvention de soi"
E. "Gentrification as the new frontier", an arrow pointing to the word "Colonization", circled twice.

Overwhelmed by possibilities, crushed under the weight of my decisions, I spend my days drinking coffee after coffee, reading frantically and walking in circles. Suicide screaming *"John John John Johnny/ He's looking so mean, he's feeling so tough, uh huh/He's looking so alive/ He's cruising the night looking for love."* Julie Doiron murmuring *"Sure is nice to see you / You look good these days/ Talking's not so easy/I wish I had more to say."* I silence my voice with the constant hum of music and the perpetual motion of my feet. I am experiencing a moment of renewal, and trying to convince myself that the life I am in the process of constructing is the life I have always wanted. I surround myself with acquaintances who all have better friends; I try to build permanence, buy my first bed, create habits, flirt with the baristas of the town's various coffee shops who only want to serve me my double espressos. I am flailing, paralyzed by insecurity, not knowing what ideas are worth sharing, knowing I have torn the fabric of my safety net by leaping and burning bridges. I am planning my lifelong exile, but I don't quite know how yet.

That summer, in the crooked apartment in Kerrytown, and then the new apartment in the Old West Side, Walter keeps me company, in the shape of a magnet of his likeness, given years ago by my old friend Alex, one of the few possessions I have carried across oceans with me. I find comfort in the magnitude of his Arcade Project and flip through its fragments, practicing bibliomancy, trying to find a path.

* * *

"To leave without being forced in any way, and to follow your inspiration as if the mere fact of turning right or turning left already constituted an essentially poetic act."
—Edmond Jaloux, "Le Dernier Flâneur," Le Temps (May 22, 1936) —Walter, pg. 436

* * *

"The masses in Baudelaire. They stretch before the flâneur as a veil: they are the newest drug for the solitary.—Second, they efface all traces of the individual: they are the newest asylum for the reprobate and the proscription.— Finally, within the labyrinth of the city, the masses are the newest and most inscrutable labyrinth. Through them, previously unknown chthonic traits are imprinted on the image of the city." —Walter, pg. 446

* * *

Every day, I walk in circles until I get dizzy, noticing the edges of the college town against my back. I am bored, lonely, hopeless. Coffee in one hand, American Spirits in the other, headphones pulled down my ears. *"I don't wanna be captured in no old romance, that passes and passes until there's no room to dance,*" sing the Fates in a cloud of mesmerizing synths. A straight line from my apartment to Comet Coffee in the Nickel Arcade, a left across from Madras Masala and another left in front of the Michigan Theater. A right towards the People's Food Co-op, until the northern edge of Kerrytown. I walk for miles every day, hoping for the movement of my feet to accelerate my fate, for my presence in the streets to create life-altering encounters. I walk miles every day because, in the movement, the feelings can be contained. I walk miles every day because movement gives me the illusion of control.

But Ann Arbor is too small, not enough room to hide the mania that has entered my body, the same mania that would possess me when the walls of my childhood bedroom would suffocate me. I dream of New York, Paris, San Francisco, Mexico City. Cities that have histories of holding bodies that look like mine, city crowds that could swallow me and spin life into luck. I dream of expansive worlds of absolute freedom, large fields of asphalt and lights, whirlwinds of movement bringing me closer to a path that fits within my skin. But in Ann Arbor, I drink coffee after coffee until my whole skin buzzes. *What will your life be? Where will you live? What will you do? Who are your people?* I have no answers, only aspirations.

* * *

As a child, I found my sense of freedom in the exploration of Mulhouse, short legs beating the cobblestone, until we had left it behind. The screams, the thumps, the fists, the bedroom doors locked to prevent us from going to school. Climbing the hills to the forest on the edge of town and hiding in the trees, until it was time to come back down, knowing that there would be consequences. Later, one mile east to Massimo's apartment where we'd smoke haschich and drink and listen to Deftones singing "*This town don't feel mine/I'm fast to get away, far,*" until I discovered that I could take trains to the capital and completely disappear within the streets of Paris. Camel cigarette in one hand, Belle and Sebastian singing "*Oh, get me away from here, I'm dying/ Play me a song to set me free*" in my ears, I would crisscross the city with the abandon of a naive child learning how to walk again. Later, a bond bought on the day of my birth, the first time there is

money, spent on a ticket to LAX. That summer of twenty-three, backpack on my shoulders, I would embody this feeling again, walking
down Market Street towards a hostel in the Mission District, the Mae
Shi screaming "*You take a bite and put it back on the shelf / We love you
better than you love yourself / It's not a bad thing to step outside of your
circle of influence if it doesn't kill you,*" in my Sennheiser headphones.
Walking under the bridge, the smell of corn and flour tortillas, the
heat of the pavement, movement and noises in a language I need to
focus to understand. My mother used to ask me what I was running
away from, not understanding it was her grip I was fleeing. Years later,
a friend would tell me "What if you're not running away from something but running towards the life you want?" and I believed him. A
life away from the claustrophobia of my upbringing, even if it required
me to yank at the roots.

* * *

"Not to find one's way in a city may well be uninteresting and banal. It
requires ignorance—nothing more. But to lose oneself in a city—as one
loses oneself in a forest—that calls for quite a different schooling. Then,
signboards and street names, passer-by, roofs, kiosk, or bars must speak
to the wanderer like a cracking twig under his feet in the forest, like the
startling call of a bittern in the distance, like the sudden stillness of a clear-
ing with a lily standing erect at its center." —Walter, "A Berlin Chronicle"

* * *

There is a magic I have only encountered, walking in cities that contain infinite layers of history and that breathe the collective air of
millions. It isn't just the electricity created by the energy of so many
bodies, it isn't just reverence towards the intricacy of architecture, it
is something else. Higher than the sum of its parts, an experience of
the sublime.

Cities create possibilities, safety, joy; they inspire the singular and
the collective. In bustling markets, overcrowded public transportation
cars, in the noise of omnipresent neighbors, I have found paths that
would never have been available otherwise. I have found family and
queerness. In the shine of street lights, the darkness of squats and bar
basements, I have encountered revelations, miraculous portals. I have

been loved. In cobblestone streets and dirt streets shared with holy animals, I learned what was kept from me behind the locked doors of my childhood. On river banks and inside museums, in used bookstores and thrift stores, I have recognized kin. I have recognized myself.

* * *

In the Fall of 2012, I fall in love and Johnny sings along to the Fates with me. Johnny doesn't crumble when I want to be alone; it's a comedy when we disagree. We lose ourselves in endless walks and conversation, the world feels wide again, Ann Arbor feels infinite; I have found the person who makes me feel both safe and free.

Three months after our first date at a Hysterics show, the fantasy ends as I retrieve an envelope from my campus mailbox. It's a letter on the university's letterhead informing me that my contract will not be renewed and that my visa will expire. No more teaching French to American students. I have two months to sell my bed, empty my apartment, break my lease, and leave the country. The walls close up again, bringing my back to the darkness of my mother's bedroom, until Johnny asks "Where should we go?" We both value pinched pennies and deep savings accounts. We have enough to last us until we figure out the next steps. That winter, we leave the depths of the Michigan winter, a school backpack each and a one-way ticket to Bangkok and I believe that in the movement I will heal it all.

Instead, I instantly fall apart. Disoriented by the shock of entering cultures I do not know, I become increasingly destabilized by the impermanent solution of our escape. In the streets, I have to adjust my rhythm to the life that permeates the sidewalks. In Phnom Penh, I drown in grief, in Hanoi I wallow at the tightness of our future. I worry that Johnny will leave after witnessing the immensity of my brokenness. For the first time, a city fails me. In Hanoi, I lose my ability to blend into crowds, and spiral into shapes of desperation. I have made a mistake coming to this corner of the world, but I don't know yet where to go next. I spend my days watching TV on the couch, air conditioning blasting, replicating the only models I have ever known. Some days, I manage to get out, and walk around Hoan Kiem lake, joining the crowds in perfect circular communion. But even the gentle lull of my walking practice doesn't soothe me. It reminds me that there is no home to return to, and that movement is the only solution. Is there a place in the world where I could softly land, is there a place in the world that can hold all of me? My mother's voice grows louder, as I fail to find my purpose.

In the darkness of that time, I thought about Walter in the unforgiving mountains of the Pyrenées, being told that he wouldn't be let into Spain and that he would be turned back to a future of concentration camps and genocide. I thought about what it means to feel like there was no place for you on this Earth anymore. That spring, I acutely understood the choices he made, because I could have made those choices too. In the narcissism of my depression, I compared my fate to his, equating my hurdles to the end of his life. I wish that Walter knew then, that the next day, they would let his people through. From Spain they boarded boats to the United States and safety. Walter's story is one I would like to rewrite. I wish that Walter knew that we would find his Arcades in George Bataille's papers, and that his words would transform the ways we understand cities. I wish that Walter knew that he helped me make sense of a world that terrified me.

When the monsoon reached Hanoi, when the water eventually swallowed the city and mimicked the heaviness of my heart, I slowly emerged. I looked for new places to be, and applied for a job at the foothills of the Annapurna mountains. A city that wasn't really one, dirt roads, water buffalos and corrugated metal roofs, in Pokhara I would remember myself by connecting to my purpose and dreams. Surrounded by teenagers who needed me to help them grow, I shed the remains of my mother's influence. In the Nepali hills I rebuilt myself anew, away from the cities that had raised me.

* * *

Flâne. A tattoo about my kinship with a man who died during his walk towards freedom from fascism in 1940. Walking from his French exile, across the Spanish border in the Pyrenees, hoping to catch a boat to America. A man who died when he realized he couldn't walk any further.

On September 25th, Walter Benjamin and his friends arrived in Portbou, a small port town at the French-Spanish border, some 30 miles south of Perpignan. They planned to cross the fascist dictatorship towards Portugal, on account of the US visa they carried. In Portugal they would board boats to freedom. But instead, after their arrival into Catalonia, their entrance was revoked and they were threatened with deportation. The next day, they would find Walter in his room of the Hotel de Francia; devoured morphine tablets accelerating his fate. He was 48 years old. The next day, the Francoist police would let his party continue their travel safely to Portugal and their boats. On October 21st 1940, Hannah Arendt would write to Gershom Sholem: "Months later, when we arrived at Portbou, we searched in vain for his grave. His name was nowhere. The cemetery looks off at a small bay, directly onto the Mediterranean. It is composed of terraces carved out of stone. The coffins are shoved into these stone walls. It is by far one of the most fantastically beautiful places I've ever seen." In his suitcase, they say he had a manuscript that disappeared. *What lessons were cut short? What did he still have to teach us, he who gave us so much already?*

* * *

In July 2013, Johnny and I board a flight filled with remittance workers returning home and a few hours later arrive in Kathmandu, greeted by the torrential rains and the mud they created. In a city as old as civilization, I practice circular walks around stupas, religious rituals sanctioned by the gods before taking a bus up and down mountains to our home for the school year, Pokhara, Nepal's tourism capital. In Pokhara, I am granted the gift of time. We move with the rhythm of seasons and scheduled power outages. We sit in the darkness, often, waiting for the lights to come back on. We read and we make shadow puppets against the wall from the headlamps we carry. I smoke Surya Golds and drink instant coffee on the balcony of the apartment facing the mountains that we share with six teenage girls. We dance to Dohori music in awkward parties we host for our small group in the empty living room. A few times a week, I walk to our office, a mile away, cutting through the small dirt path I share with water buffalos, the Talking Heads rhythming my feet as David Byrne sings *"The highways and cars/Were sacrificed for agriculture /I thought that we'd start over /But I guess I was wrong."* Every week or so, Johnny and I walk the few miles that separate us from the tourist strip, Lakeside, where we stay the night in a cheap hostel to access hot water. Sometimes, the loadshedding happens as the night falls, and we walk alone in the deserted streets, enveloped by a sky filled with bright stars.

We are a six-hour drive away from Kathmandu, in a landlocked country. In the deep isolation of this life, somewhat removed from capitalism, my nervous system settles, I am able to imagine another life.

* * *

"Life within the magic circle of eternal return makes for an existence that never emerges from the auratic." —Walter, pg. 119

* * *

Flâne as a lifestyle, I guess, or as a political commitment maybe. The promise to move at the speed of my feet, and to let myself experience the magic that this world can grant. The holiness of the unplanned, the cycles of rebirth that come from experiencing new realities. *Flâne* as a commitment to myself and my sovereignty, the belief that no matter what forces try to control me, there is power in walking. *Flâne* as queerness, the perpetual devotion to the unfolding. *Flâne* as the miracle of a life built from the rubbles of a traumatic childhood, in the messy ways that rebuilding sometimes requires. *Flâne*, as an ode to the fire and the spleen. It's no coincidence that in the summer of 2012 I thought about Walter Benjamin as I decided to jump ship and let myself freefall. A man who I always shared imaginary kinship with, who died at the edge of freedom. *What if he had made it to safety?*

Heavenly Tree

THE CRUELTY OF AMERICA CONTINUES TO SURPRISE ME, AFTER years of visiting jails, hospitals, shelters and hospices. I thought I had seen all the different ways systems degrade and destroy. Yet I had to force myself to not collapse as I walked past the inhabited cells of the oldest prison of our state.

It was a spring day, and we had woken up at dawn to make it on time to our event, set to take place in the gym, an event organized by a man serving a life sentence between those walls. We were an odd group of organizers, mismatched in age, race and class, but we were invited to talk about our fight to end life without parole in our state; the mandatory sentence for those convicted of killing others. We were asked to do so by men who languished behind the walls of this haunted dungeon, built in 1889 as Reformatory for Young Offenders, that has since then become a close-security facility along the Juniata River.

It is a rare sight to enter the living quarters of a prison, as newer buildings are designed to prevent such lifting of the veil to those who don't inhabit those places. Guided by an activity manager, we walked past Dickensian cells, made of coils of metals, covered by their inhabitants with sheets hung to create a semblance of privacy.

But a quick peek would reveal objects accumulated and lives lived. Makeshift kettles, piles of books, socks hanging on the bars to dry. The mundanity of every life, a reminder of the ways humans adapt to their conditions.

Around us, solemn groups of men walking in neat lines, cast fast glances at our party, forbidden to interact with us by the laws regulating the place. In the prison gym, after the few yards that felt like endless miles, we were greeted by a hundred men wearing larger than needed browns, stamped with white letters. DOC. Department of Corrections. A sea of Black and Brown faces, some of them requiring wheelchairs and canes to join us, some of them so old that their presence jolted my bones.

I never had a neat origin story of my abolitionist world views, only the memory of the penitentiary of my hometown, a stone edifice wrapped in barbed wire, the firm grip of my parents and my own experiences of internment. I have always understood the need for freedom; I have never believed in the punishment of restriction and in that prison, planted in rural Pennsylvania, I fought the fantasy of unlocking all the doors, of crowds of liberty running to the hills and safety.

* * *

In 1784, William Hamilton of Philadelphia, an avid plant collector, son of Andrew, brought in a few seeds of Chinese trees to his home of the Woodlands on the banks of the Schuykill river. Part of a network of men who paid large amounts of money to acquire plants from countries they couldn't colonize yet, he received the seeds by way of a French missionary. A *Gingko Bilboa* and an *Ailanthus Altissima*, known in the Lower Yellow River region of China as Ch'un Shu, meaning Spring Tree in English, called colloquially Tree of Heaven.

In colonial America, William Hamilton would grow the Tree of Heaven, praising it for its fast growth (5 feet a year!), and the ways it would bend over pedestrians and create elegant canopies of shade. By the mid-19th century, the celestial tree would be available in nurseries all around the land. And when they cut the lindens in the 1840s because of worm infestations, they replaced them with the Ailanthus trees whose scent was so strong that no bug would attack its bark. The Ailanthus tree invaded American cities, despite the unpleasant wafts it would unleash on their sidewalks.

How could William Hamilton know that his practice of bringing plants that didn't belong would have such dire consequences? How could he know that in the following centuries the Tree of Heaven would dominate the land he colonized?

* * *

In the summer and fall of 2019, the spotted lanternflies (*Lycorma Delicatula*) swarmed the Philadelphia area. Biblical plagues of modern times. Insects hailing from China, so beautiful that they felt menacing, the lanternflies would fall from the sky, latch on to trees and destroy the crops. The newspaper would report messages from state officials asking the public to kill them, so, many did. Reports of stores closing because of infestations, sidewalks covered in their squished bodies, the lanternflies took over the landscape of the city and our imaginations.

That summer of the plagues, I would walk in and out of the closest state prison on a biweekly basis to facilitate workshops about trauma, created at the request of friends of a friend. I taught a six-month certification course, mostly to men serving life sentences that I called Trauma and Reentry. Conversations about shame and neglect, about the traumatic effect of poverty and glimmers of hope in the sterile box of an American penitentiary. We would meet in the maze of the education wing, in a gray room overlooking the yard. Fifteen men seated on chairs too small, who created community and safety together. We shared stories of pain and survival and we laughed together, discussing the future that their sentences prevented. I would play along with their hopes of freedom, preparing them for the difficulties they would be facing if the doors of the prison opened and closed at their back.

The prison, built amongst the fields of suburban Philadelphia, sat on the grounds of an older prison, shut down a few years before. Named after the immortal bird, the front desk was surrounded by a mural of a phoenix rising from its ashes. A strange legacy to boast.

That summer of the plagues, as we walked through the yard, surrounded by men who only wanted to heal, the spotted lanternflies would flop on our bodies, unbothered. Grown men, proud men shrank terrified of the small creatures. Despite the government's invective, the men walking the prison yard could not kill the lanternflies, because they had been labeled murderers, psychopaths, antisocial, and if they killed, then, the diagnosis would be true. A summer of anxiety, forcing them to inaction in the face of discomfort, the lanternflies testing the limits of our humanity, forcing me to reckon with who gets to kill under the sun of capitalism.

* * *

On a scorching week of August, I spend my days in front of my computer, lulled to infinite joy by the brilliance of queers from all over the country. It's a virtual writing retreat for emerging artists and I spend it in a small post-industrial town on the unceded land of the Pequot people, in the empty apartment of a friend. One of those American towns where the sidewalks are sparse and the Main Street emptied. The lack of options brings me back to versions of myself I had thought shed a decade ago, as I walk along the road to buy water from the gas station. The white supremacist wafts emanating from the thin blue line flags scare me, so I keep the volume in my headphones louder than needed and regret my choice to pack colorful clothes, hot pink and bright yellow pants, cobalt blues and teal shirts.

But it doesn't matter too much, I am writing, reading, listening. In between sessions, I walk along the river, and try to silence the anxious voices of solitude by observing my surroundings, paying attention to what grows and what doesn't. It is a disturbed landscape. Mugwort, sumac and tree of heaven grow abundantly in between well-manicured lawns claimed by star-spangled flags.

Sometimes that week, as I refresh my phone on one of my walks, I learn that Albert Woodfox died. I learn it on Twitter, and for a moment imagine worlds where death still holds sacredness. Albert Woodfox, one of the Angola 3, spent forty-four years in the solitary confinement of the former plantation of Angola turned deadly penitentiary. Until he walked to freedom, wrote a book, traveled across the country to tell us about his life.

As my feet continue to propel me forward, I try to think about ways to memorialize his existence. Taken by COVID-19, like Clarence before him, like Reem. Men who survived until another plague took them away. Dante tells me that he survived the plague because he survived drinking the water of the penitentiary that saw his best years wasted away. I somehow can't find the tears, just fields of Tree of Heaven and gratitude for Albert's generosity.

* * *

In my garden, I spend cool fall mornings seeding the plants of the following season. The backyard is an exercise in humility, as I take inventory of all the plants that grow there, uninvited by my hands. Plantain, fleabane, Norway maple saplings and Tree of Heaven. I crouch and pull but restrain myself in the presence of the *Ailanthus*.

Tree of Heaven is labeled as invasive because of its ability to grow in the poorest of soil. A greatly adaptive plant, it spreads allelopathic chemicals that prevent other plants from growing in its vicinity. If pulled, the plant will grow deeper roots underground, roots that are so creative that they are able to materialize fifty feet from the main plant. There aren't many ways to kill the Tree of Heaven that don't, instead, make it grow stronger. The *Ailanthus'* underground life is a network of runners, moving farther and farther from each other, until one root builds a forest. Unless you pour chemicals that will seep into the soil and affect the rest of the ecosystem. I am not ready.

A friend recommends I cut the plant close to the soil and cover the remaining stump in a plastic bag to suffocate it and prevent more growth, a technique she heard from an arborist relative. A few weeks after I duct taped grocery bags around what is left of the tree, more pop up, growing defiantly under my incredulous eyes. Can I contain the Trees of Heaven without dousing them in poison that would prevent all life to grow? Can I enter a relationship of trust with them?

* * *

"KILL THE INVADER."

In the streets of Philadelphia, flyers were posted on poles warning us about the danger of the spotted lanternflies, disruptors of capitalist agriculture. Pictures of their delicate polka-dotted bodies, and the reminder that they were attracted to vines, specifically the bark of the *Ailanthus Altissima*.

Once attached to a tree, the lanternflies will suck its sap and secrete a sugary substance, called honeydew that will in turn produce mold. The honeydew destroys the plant that hosted the lanternfly. Fruit trees, vines, and crops die in the presence of the spotted winged invader, and especially dire problem in a landscape of monocultures.

"Smash them, smash them!" On the edge of the trail of the forested preserve, a family of four is excitingly killing lanternflies. The parents chant as their children squish small bodies into oblivion. I have been smashing lanternflies too and, in that moment, I question my choices. Heat rises in my body, the shame of my ignorance faced with the concrete mirror of my decisions.

* * *

In 1797, the Quakers of Philadelphia practice an experiment. What if, instead of forcing bodies into cells with others, those who have harmed others are made to sit alone to repent for their actions. In the Walnut Street Prison of Philadelphia they build small cells with high ceilings containing a bed, a water tap and a privy pipe. Preventing communication with the outside world and each other, the cells are meant to be a space of quiet reflection. This model, known as the Philadelphia model will soon be replicated in the Eastern State Penitentiary, before spreading into what we currently know as solitary confinement, a torturous practice that destroys the human mind.

How could the Quakers know that their idea of repentance would have such dire consequences? How could the Quakers know that, in the following centuries, the practice of solitary confinement would become so pervasive? Why do I assign them innocence?

* * *

The Tree of Heaven is now ubiquitous on Turtle Island, having spread around urban communities and into long-established forests. In Pennsylvania, it mixes with the eastern white pine and the gray birch, adapting itself to the Delaware Water Gap. In Philadelphia, it is the 4th most represented tree in the urban canopy, mixing with the black cherry, boxelder, ash, and northern white cedar trees. It is found on some of the oldest streets of the city, as well as on the side of the road and railways.

In the summer, when the sidewalk explodes with green, the Tree of Heaven grows between the cracks of cement, until it produces the fruit or samara that will contain so many seeds that it could rebuild worlds.

They say that the Tree of Heaven was introduced on three different occasions on Turtle Island, first in Philadelphia by William Hamilton, then New York to replace the lindens, and eventually brought to California by Chinese railroad workers and gold miners, transporting some of their ancestral medicine to their new homes. They planted the trees along the streams, to harvest their bounty and recreate semblances of familiarity in this foreign land.

In China, we find the *Ailanthus* referenced in the Tang Dynasty's Materia Medica compiled in 656 A.D, meaning that the people there would use its part for their medicine. They'd say that one could make a decoction of its roots to support those believed to be possessed by demons; that its leaves, slightly poisonous, could calm the nervous system. Practitioners of Chinese medicine might also recommend the root to help a damp-heat condition, possibly causing dysentery, intestinal hemorrhage or menorrhagia. In 1596, Li Shih-Chen would publish the Pen Ts'ao Kang Mu, a pivotal document in the history of Chinese medicine. In it, he'd describe many recipes using the ailanthus to cure ailments, mostly of intestinal nature.

In 2018, in an article titled "Antitumor Activity of the *Ailanthus Altissima* Bark Phytochemical Ailanthone against Breast Cancer MCF-7 cells" Ruxing Wang would highlight the cancer treatment ability of the Tree of Heaven. The Tree of Heaven, Spring Tree, more than its ability to spread, more than its ability to invade. A complicated life.

* * *

Today, on Turtle Island, it's estimated that 80,000 people are living in solitary confinement at any given time. Special Housing Units (SHU), the hole, administrative segregation, supermax prisons, all different names for the practice of placing an individual into a cell, often compared in size to a bathroom, without any contact with the outside world. Six feet by nine feet. Food is served in trays, slid through the cell door, walls are thick to avoid communication between people held in the same unit. Most people who have lived in solitary confinement will describe the unending screams, the constant thump of human activity, the excrements on the walls. They will tell you about the people hearing voices, the soft whimper of cries, the dehumanization. They will tell you about the dog runs, small cages in which you are allowed to exercise outside for an hour a day without other humans around you. Many will tell you that to survive they had to duplicate their mind, disconnect from the body forced into the site. Many will tell you, later, after they're home, of the nightmares that occur in the dark of the night, of their tendency to isolate when things get hard, the difficulty to trust others. I see the eyes darting in discomfort around other bodies; the constant need to prove that the torture didn't break anything. I see the consequences of choices, meant to harm, without any innocence in sight.

* * *

If they stopped cutting the grass of prison yards across the state of Pennsylvania, if they stopped spraying the lawns with chemicals preventing plants from growing, the Trees of Heaven might be some of the first ones to erupt. Along with the ragweed and asters, the *Ailanthus* would take over, creating canopies of shade while eating away at the foundation of cement. Progressively weakening the base, until it would all collapse. And in its aftermath, I want to believe that other species would follow, blackberries and raspberry, cherry trees and black birch.

The forest is always waiting to take over, and in my chest sits the dreams of each penitentiary being swallowed by branches and leaves. In my chest lies the belief that some day, the buildings of torture and destruction will disappear in the thick of green life. No more boxes of isolation, no more state issued clothing, no more over processed food. Jungles of *Ailanthus*, devouring the foundations of a system meant to destroy; the *Ailanthus* finding an opponent its size and spreading its roots far and wide until there isn't an enemy to fight anymore, incapable of rising from its ashes again.

* * *

In Washington DC, on a late summer day, when the crisp air carries a coming fall, I share a cigarette with Henry, sentenced to life in 1963. "They told me I would die in that penitentiary." The penitentiary, Angola, the former plantation turned largest prison on Turtle Island. Larger than Manhattan, in West Feliciana Parish surrounded on three sides by the mighty Mississippi river.

Outside of the hotel, he was sitting alone before I approached him and he admitted not knowing how to buy cigarettes in this city he was seeing for the first time. "You are Mr. Montgomery, aren't you?" I had said, overwhelmed by the memories of my tears flowing that morning. Earlier that day I had watched him stand in a full room that erupted in tearful claps to celebrate him. His children, some two hundred adults, who had also been sentenced to die in prison in their youth, are also home now, because of a Supreme Court ruling brought in by his staunch attempts at finding the key to freedom. His stubbornness forced retroactive application of a law forbidding automatic life sentences to minors. Cruel and unusual punishment. I had been invited to the gathering to provide support for those triggered by the moment, but I mostly spent my days catching up with old friends.

His face breaks into wide smiles as he shares life out in the world. He's now 76, freed last fall. The father of a movement.

"Stubborn dreamer," I tease him through the cloud of his hearing aids and his large smile returns. He tells stories of freedom imagined in the depth of cotton fields that used to be harvested by the enslaved hands of people sold from the borders of the country of Angola, now replaced by the hands of men subjected to the cruelty because of the 13th amendment. Bodies replaced, stories repeated.

In the depth of the plantation they tried to kill him. Young child from Louisiana now living in a hotel room in the Delta, he is free, gathering the roses growing from all the seeds he planted.

Stubborn dreamers painting words where the roots of trees of heaven could crack the foundation of every building that brings death. Just like the Banyan swallowing the temples of Angkor Wat, the Trees of Heaven will dig into the foundations of the Empire until they crack.

In Louisiana, on Houma land, the *Ailanthus* grows too and I imagine it progressively eating at the crops of oppression grown on a land first enslaved and then incarcerated: wheat, corn, soybeans, cotton and milo.

The Tree of Heaven's miraculous properties will one day take over this land of the Empire, dousing it with honeydew until nothing but forests of canopies grow, slowly eroding the slave quarters turned prison cells. Stubborn dreamers will dance as the gates of solitude and desperation are progressively turned into dust by the natural forces they are trying to ignore. We will win freedom for all, in the shape of forests of trees displaced by the greed of men; we will win freedom for all in the fields of green leaves slowly consuming the heart of Empires. And when we do, when thousands walk their path towards the healing of ancestral wounds, we will dance, together, singing the songs of our collective liberations. We will win freedom for all, for the children of sharecroppers, the children of the Philadelphia streets, the children who they wanted to kill. We will win freedom for all, and erect structures of connection. Together, after all.

Acknowledgments

In December 2021, a day before hopping on a plane to Mexico, I decided to submit *The Land is Holy* to a contest organized by Radix knowing that Hanif Abdurraqib would be reading the finalists' work. That's all I wanted: my favorite living author to see my words. I am immensely grateful to have been chosen as the winner of the Megaphone Prize. To the entirety of the Radix team, to Hanif Abdurraqib for offering me a chance at publication: Thank you for teaching me that there is no ceiling to joy.

To my editor Meher Manda, who has read endless versions of prickly essays: Thank you for fighting for my words.

Thank you to my *Catapult* essay generator workshop. Febo, Frankie, LJ, Kim, Rasha, Elizabeth—you were my first readers, and your feedback immensely impacted my writing practice. To Hannah Harris-Sutro, my writing companion, the friend I didn't expect to make: your brilliance has shaped this manuscript in too many ways to name and I hope we'll have many more years of weekly Zooms together. Eternal gratitude to the incredible Kai Cheng Thom for teaching me that I had a voice worth listening to.

Deep gratitude to Molly who knew I was writing a book well before I did.

Lambda Literary Retreat for Queer Writers was the first space where I understood myself as a writer. Thank you to the fierce Edgar Gomez for telling me I was one, and thank you to everybody in my workshop. Being in spaces of unapologetic queer literature opened so many possibilities into this text. Eternal gratitude to the Lambda staff, especially to dear, dear Chloe Feffer. To years of mischief ahead.

Many essays in this collection are inspired by the work of my friend Layla Feghali. Thank you for your gifts, for being the Cancer to my Capricorn, for teaching us to look at the past with reverence and rigor. May we re-root ourselves at the crossroads in all the lifetimes to come.

Thank you to the Re-membrance circle people including Aziz, Isa, Iman, Deema, Vadi. Thank you to Amirah for your friendship.

To the Radius of Arab American Writers (RAWI) for the support, with a special thanks to Summer Farah.

To the plants and the plant teachers including the Build Your Home Apothecary crew and the SHAREHerbs family. To my many plant teachers, thank you for continuing to tend to the land and to sow seeds of the worlds we want to see.

Many gratitudes to *Foglifter* for publishing "Fruits of the Desert" in issue 8.1. To Tauheed Zaman, for inviting me to grow my writing practice, for the friendship and the writing club.

Thank you to Sarah Clark for giving me the fastest acceptance for "Thinking about na3na3" and publishing the piece in *ALOCASIA*. Thank you to the *ANMLY* family for being a sweet writing home.

Thank you to the staff at *The Massachusetts Review*, especially Jenzo Duque and Edward Clifford for believing in "Freedom Trees."

Thank you to Lance Cleland and A.L. Major at the Tin House workshop, to Cyrus Dunham and all the writers I was lucky to meet there.

Deep gratitude to Nicole Shawan Junior and Vanessa Mártir for the beautiful Roots Wounds.Words retreat where I learned that maybe I was a poet and that maybe I could fall in love with my entire workshop.

To the poets in disguise: Dr. Camille U. Adams, Dr. Cecilia Caballero, Celeste Chan, Desiree Browne, Elina Zhang, Flávia Monteiro, Mayookh Barua, Misha Ponnuraju, Phillip Dwight Morgan, SG Huerta, Victoria Lagunas, and to the poetest of poets himself Marcelo Hernandez Castillo, I love you all deeply and will spend a lifetime looking for words to express the ways meeting you changed me. Thank you for the biweekly workshops filled with diagrams, laughter, tears, gentle pushes, and deep vulnerability. What an absolute privilege to be your friend.

To Donia Salem Harhoor, sweet poet kin, thank you for always feeling like home.

To the luminous Aisha Sabatini Sloan and Jaquira Diaz, to the entirety of my Sewanee nonfiction workshop: Ebony Haight, Max Pasakorn, Elena Dudum, Dr. Jennifer DeClue, Brooke McKinney, Amy Evans, April Yee, Emily Prado, Katoya Ellis Fleming, Milena Nigam, Joe Osdmunson. What a miracle to be read, understood, pushed, and celebrated by such a smart, caring group of people. To Leah Stewart, Gwen Kirby, and Adam Latham, to the brilliant faculty.

To the friends I made that summer including Cindy Juyoung Ok, Yassmin Abdel-Magied, Dr. Yvette DeChavez. To Cory Calabria, who I have met in many lives before this one, I cherish your existence.

To my Pocoapoco family, thank you for making it possible for me to come back to Oaxaca. Dafne, Fernanda, Jessica, Aurelia, Evelyn, I will always admire the world you have created, and I am grateful for all the ways I get to be part of it. Isaac, Aria, and Adinah, thank you for being home for two weeks.

Thank you to Neda Haffari and Jupiter Pradhan for inviting me into Space A in Kathmandu. To Niranjan Kunwar, may we queer all the land. To Muna Gurung for becoming instant kin.

To my Kaalo family, to Helena, both the softest and fiercest Naga the world has known. Beloved Aquarius, thank you for being family.

To Momo, I will always love you.

I wouldn't have made it through this process without the support of the Periplus collective and more specifically the support of my mentor Grace Talusan, who continues to teach me how to be ferociously attuned to my feelings and wounds without sacrificing my dignity. Thank you for your generosity, your friendship, your voice. Thank you for teaching me what it looks like to be part of this literary community. I aspire to be like you someday.

In an industry that wants us to believe in constant scarcity, Periplus has been a space of resistance, of shared ideas and resources. Eternal gratitude to Vauhini Vara and Pia Owens. To the writers I've been honored to interview including Daniel Peña, Zeyn Joukhadar, Jami Nakamura Lin, Dina Nayeri, Dustin Pearson. To the millions of group chats, conversations with my Peripals including Anes Ahmed, Nathan Xie, jonah wu, aureleo sans, and benedict nguyen. To Sara Montijo for the lyre serenades and city escapades.

To my Center family, to Petty D, to TreeTree, to every one of my friends in the dungeons, until all the walls fall. To the real Shyeed, who I miss every day, we will meet again. To Henry Montgomery, Eddie, Abdallah, Saleem, Sharif, John, Suave, Ghani, thank you for freeing us each day.

To Alison and TJ, thank you for teaching me how to transmute my angst. Thank you for giving me the gift of freedom.

Throughout the process of writing this book, many people carried me in different ways, including healers, bodyworkers, care workers. In a world where feminized labor is invisibilized, I want to celebrate the people who have (literally) held me: Alice, Cara, Celeste, Dori, Jennye, Jo, Lore, Mo, Nasrene, Rose, Sonalee.

To the original Jo, thank you for a decade of friendship and birds. To my life partner Annike who has taught me about the many shapes unconditional love can take. To a lifetime of being the butch to your femme.

And to you, Johnny, who has always seen me for who I am now. I don't even know what life would have been without you. Beloved introverted triple fire, thank you for all the quiet years and thank you for being so joyful at the idea of sharing me with the world.

To the smaller version of me, the child version of me, the kid who didn't think they'd make it past fifteen, eighteen, twenty-seven, thirty. Thank you for surviving.

To the stubborn dreamers, we will win.

Bibliography

A LIFE IN FLIGHT

The Egyptian Soul: The Ka, the Ba, and the Akh, myweb.usf.edu/~liottan/theegyptian-soul.html.

Arizaga, Juan, et al. "Importance of Artificial Stopover Sites through Avian Migration Flyways: A landfill-based Assessment with the White Stork Ciconia Ciconia." Ibis (London, England), vol. 160, no. 3, 2018, pp. 542-553.

Chernetsov, Nikita & Berthold, Peter & Querner, Ulrich. (2004). Migratory orientation of first-year White Storks (Ciconia ciconia): inherited information and social interactions. The Journal of experimental biology. 207. 937-43. 10.1242/jeb.00853.

Margolis, Marvin, and Philip Parker. "The Stork Fable—Some Psychodynamic Considerations." Journal of the American Psychoanalytic Association, vol. 20, no. 3, July 1972, pp. 494–511, doi:10.1177/000306517202000304.

Mark, Joshua J. "The Soul in Ancient Egypt." *World History Encyclopedia*, https://www.worldhistory.org#organization, 6 Sept. 2023, www.worldhistory.org/article/1023/the-soul-in-ancient-egypt/.

Mikołaj Czajkowski, Marek Giergiczny, Jakub Kronenberg, Piotr Tryjanowski. The economic recreational value of a white stork nesting colony: A case of 'stork village' in Poland, Tourism Management, Volume 40, 2014, Pages 352-360,

Watts, Linda S. "The Stork." American Myths, Legends, and Tall Tales: An Encyclopedia of American Folklore, edited by Christopher R. Fee and Jeffrey B. Webb, vol. 3, ABC-CLIO, 2016, pp. 897-900.

THE MALLARDS

"Birding in the United States: A Demographic and Economic Analysis Addendum to the 2006 National Survey of Fishing, Hunting, and Wildlife-Associated Recreation" (2009). US Fish & Wildlife Publications. 164. https://digitalcommons.unl.edu/usfwspubs/164

Catalano, Robin. "Could a Birding Boom in the U.S. Help Conservation Take Flight?" Travel, National Geographic, 2 Sept. 2021, www.nationalgeographic.com/travel/article/could-a-boom-in-us-birding-help-fund-conservation?loggedin-=true&rnd=1677629341937

The AOUDADS

"Barbary Sheep." Details, Texas Invasive Species Institute, www.tsusinvasives.org/home/database/ammotragus-lervia. Accessed 22 Aug. 2022.

Bounaceur, Farid, et al. "Is there a future for the last populations of aoudad (Ammotragus lervia) in northern Algeria?." Pakistan journal of zoology 48.6 (2016): 1727-1731.

Boum, Aomar. Memories of Absence: How Muslims Remember Jews in Morocco. Stanford University Press, 2013.

Cassinello, J. "Ammotragus lervia (aoudad). Invasive species compendium." (2015).

Cassinello, J., Bounaceur, F., Brito, J.C., Bussière, E., Cuzin, F., Gil-Sánchez, J., HerreraSánchez, F. & Wacher, T. 2021. Ammotragus lervia. The IUCN Red List of Threatened Species 2021: e.T1151A22149987. https://dx.doi.org/10.2305/IUCN.UK.2021-3.RLTS.T1151A22149987.en
Gottreich, Emily. The Mellah of Marrakesh: Jewish and Muslim Space in Morocco's Red City. Indiana University Press, 2007.

Gottreich, Emily Benichou, and Daniel J. Schroeter, eds. Jewish culture and society in North Africa. Indiana University Press, 2011.

Gottreich, Emily Benichou. Morocco: A Jewish History from Pre-Islamic to Post-Colonial Times. I.B. Tauris, 2020.

Ouchaou B et al. "Les Grands Mammifères Disparus Du Maroc Durant L'holocène." Anthropologie (France) V 121 N 1-2 (2017 05 01): 133-145 2017 https://doi.org/10.1016/j.anthro.2017.03.021.

PANOUSE Jean B. Les Mammifères Du Maroc. *Primates Carnivores Pinnipèdes Artiodactyles. Par J.b. Panouse...Avec...Un Glossaire Des Noms Indigènes En Collaboration Avec L. Galand.* 1957.

Renault, Marion. "Texas Can't Quit the Aoudad." *The Atlantic*, 13 Jan. 2020, https://www.theatlantic.com/science/archive/2020/01/how-aoudad-invaded-texas/604834/.

Simpson CD. "Symposium on ecology and management of Barbary Sheep". Texas Tech. Univ. press, Lubbock. 1980

Temime, Émile, and Nathalie Deguigné. *Le Camp Du Grand Arénas: Marseille, 1944-1966.* Éd. Autrement, 2001.

Yoakum, Jim. "First Barbary Sheep Symposium." Wildlife Society Bulletin (1973-2006), vol. 8, no. 1, 1980, pp. 87–88. JSTOR, http://www.jstor.org/stable/3781390.

THINKING ABOUT NA3NA3

Cornwell, Graham Hough. Sweetening the Pot: A History of Tea and Sugar in Morocco, 1850-1960. Georgetown University, 2018.

"FAOSTAT." Fao.org, 2022, www.fao.org/faostat/fr/#rankings/countries_by_commodity. Pickering, Victoria. Mint: The Ubiquity of a Commercial Crop. Dumbarton Oaks,Plant Humanities, 2022.

FRUITS OF THE DESERT

Abufarha, Nasser. "Land of symbols: Cactus, poppies, orange and olive trees in Palestine." Identities, vol. 15, no. 3, 2008, pp. 343–368, https://doi.org/10.1080/10702890802073274.

Ayyash, Mark Muhannad. "An Assemblage of decoloniality? Palestinian Fellahin resistance and the space-place relation." Studies in Social Justice 12.1 (2018): 21-37.

Bardenstein, Carol. "Threads of Memory and Discourses of Rootedness: Of Trees, Oranges and the Prickly-Pear Cactus in Israel/Palestine." Edebiyât, vol. 8, no. 1, 1998, pp. 1.

Davis, Rochelle. "1. Geographies of dispossession". Palestinian Village Histories: Geographies of the Displaced, Redwood City: Stanford University Press, 2010, pp. 1-26. https://doi-org.proxy.library.upenn.edu/10.1515/9780804777186-005

Ghédira, K., and P. Goetz. "Figuier de barbarie: Opuntia ficus-indica (Cactaceae)." Phytothérapie 16.6 (2018): 374.

Jiménez, Erika. "'The occupation wants to delete us': Palestinian youth's interpretations of and resistance to settler colonialism." Third World Quarterly, 2023, pp. 1–19, https://doi.org/10.1080/01436597.2023.2230901.

Labro, Camille. Le Monde, 8 Oct. 2018, https://www.lemonde.fr/m-gastronomie/article/2018/10/08/la-figue-de-barbarie-un-fruit-piquant_5366323_4497540.html.

"Prisoners' Lawyer: Zakaria Zubeidi Was Severely Beaten after Arrest, Suffers from Broken Jaws, Ribs." The Palestine Chronicle, 15 Sept. 2021, https://www.palestinechronicle.com/prisoners-lawyer-zakaria-zubeidi-was-severely-beaten-after-arrest-suffers-from-broken-jaws-ribs/.

Route 18, Fragments of a Journey in Palestine-Israel. Directed by Michel Khleifi, Eyal Sivan, Memento Films, 2003

"THE FIFTH INTERNATIONAL CONGRESS OF ZIONISTS." The American Jewish Year Book, vol. 4, 1902, pp. 78–86. JSTOR, http://www.jstor.org/stable/23600078.

"The First Decade: 1901-1910 - Keren Kayemeth Leisrael - KKL-JNF." KKL-JNF, www.kkl-jnf.org/second_decade_1901_1910/.

TOI Staff. "PM Said Looking at Special Task-Force to Nationalize KKL-JNF." The Times of Israel, 27 Dec. 2017, https://www.timesofisrael.com/pm-said-looking-at-special-task-force-to-nationalize-the-jnf/.

PLANTE PERSISTANTE

Adrian Boas, and Rabei G. Khamisy. Montfort : History, Early Research and Recent Studies of the Principal Fortress of the Teutonic Order. Brill, 2016.

'Artemisia arborescens', CABI Compendium. CABI. doi: 10.1079/cabicompendium.112439, 2022

Boccaccio Giovanni et al. Concerning Famous Women. George Allen & Unwin 1964

Feghali, Layla. "What Does 'Plantcestor' Mean?" Ancestral HUB | reCollecting Our Stories Home, 21 Apr. 2016, swanaancestralmedicinehub.wordpress.com/2015/03/11/what-does-plantcestor-mean/.

Greenwalt, William S. "Artemisia II (c. 395–351 BCE)." Women in World History: A Biographical Encyclopedia, edited by Anne Commire, vol. 1, Yorkin Publications, 2002, pp. 509-514.

Jaradat, Nidal, et al. "Assessing artemisia arborescens essential oil compositions, antimicrobial, cytotoxic, anti-inflammatory, and neuroprotective effects gathered from two geographic locations in Palestine." Industrial Crops and Products, vol. 176, 2022, p. 114360, https://doi.org/10.1016/j.indcrop.2021.114360.

Moldenke, Harold N, and Alma L Moldenke. *Plants of the Bible*. New York: Ronald Press Co., 1952.

Wright Colin W. Artemisia. Taylor & Francis 2002.

A SMALL CORRECTION ABOUT SPOONS AND BIRDS

"Last Two Escaped Palestinian Prisoners Surrender to Israel Forces." *Al Jazeera*, 19 Sept. 2021, https://www.aljazeera.com/news/2021/9/19/last-two-escaped-palestinian-prisoners-recaptured-israeli-police.

Tee Grizzley. "First Day Out", A Moment. 300 Entertainment, 2017. MP3.
I borrowed the syntax of this line "after the pre-trials, after the status/ After them impact statements, after the castle"

MY MOTHER'S MOTHER

Bilu, Yoram, and Henry Abramovitch. "In search of the Saddiq: Visitational dreams among Moroccan Jews in Israel." *Psychiatry* 48.1 (1985): 83-92.

IN THE SHADOW OF HIS BODY

Auerhahn, N. C. & Prelinger, E. (1983) Repetition in the Concentration Camp Survivor and her Child. International Review of Psychoanalysis 10:31-46

"Base de données centrales des noms des victimes de la Shoah". *Yadvashem.org*, 2023, yvng.yadvashem.org/index.html?language=fr.

"Convoi N° 61 Du 28 Octobre 1943." *Les Déportés Juifs de La Sarthe*, les déportés juifs de la Sarthe, 10 Mar. 2015, lesdeportesdesarthe.wordpress.com/convoi-n-61-du-28-octobre-1943/.

Daltroff, Jean, and Christophe Hamm. *La Route Du Judaïsme En Alsace : Un Itinéraire À Travers L'histoire, Les Traditions Et Le Patrimoine*. Rosheim: ID l'édition, 2006.

Ephraim Max. Histoire des Juifs d'Alsace et particulièrement de Strasbourg depuis le milieu du XIIIe jusqu'à la fin du XIVe siècle (suite et fin). In: Revue des études juives, tome 78, n°155-156, janvier-juin 1924. pp. 35-84; https://www.persee.fr/doc/rjuiv_0484-8616_1924_num_78_155_5428

Global Volcanism Program, 2023. Mount Vesuvius (211020) in [Database] Volcanoes of the World (v. 5.1.1; 17 Aug 2023). Distributed by Smithsonian Institution, compiled by Venzke, E. https://doi.org/10.5479/si.GVP.VOTW5-2023.5.1

"Holocaust Survivors and Victims Database " *Ushmm.org*, 2019, https://www.ushmm. org/remember/resources-holocaust-survivors-victims

Lerch Dominique, Raphaël Freddy. Le colportage juif en Alsace au XIXe siècle. In: Revue des sciences sociales de la France de l'Est, Hors-Série, 1977. L'Alsace rurale. pp. 102-119; doi : https://doi.org/10.3406/revss.1977.3623 https://www.persee.fr/doc/revss_0336-1578_1977_hos_1_1_3623

"Liste Des Convois de France." Yadvashem.org, 2023, www.yadvashem.org/fr/recherche/convois-de-france.html.

Pliny VI:16 cited in Dougal Jerram, et al. *Volcanoes of Europe*. Dunedin Academic Press, 2017. p 27

Schwarzfuchs, Simon, and Jean-Luc Fray. *Présence Juive En Alsace Et Lorraine Médiévales : Dictionnaire De Géographie Historique*. Paris: Les éditions du Cerf, 2015.

The Encyclopedia of Volcanoes, edited by Haraldur Sigurdsson, et al., Elsevier Science & Technology, 2015. ProQuest Ebook Central, http://ebookcentral.proquest.com/lib/upenn-ebooks/detail.action?docID=1983593.

Weill Georges. Recherches sur la démographie des Juifs d'Alsace du XVIe au XVIIIe siècle. In: Revue des études juives, tome 130, n°1, janvier-mars 1971. pp. 51-90; https://www.persee.fr/doc/rjuiv_0484-8616_1971_num_130_1_1674

FREEDOM TREES

Brown, Terry. "The Duke of Sully and His Trees." *The Duke of Sully and His Trees*, sullystrees.weebly.com/.

Fechner, Erik. "L'arbre de la liberté: objet, symbole, signe linguistique." *Mots. Les langages du politique* 15.1 (1987): 23-42.

Gadant, Jean. "Les arbres du souvenir et de la Liberté." *Revue forestière française* 41.5 (1989): 439-444.

Grégoire, Henri Jean-Baptiste. Essai historique et patriotique sur les arbres de la liberté, présenté par le représentant Grégoire, lors de la séance du 12 germinal an II (1er avril 1794). In: Tome LXXXVII - Du 1er au 12 germinal An II (21 mars au 1er avril 1794) pp. 670-680.

Krinitiz, Esther. Esther and the Dream of One Loving Human Family *February 23 2019-March 3 2024, American Visionary Art Museum*, Baltimore

"Linden Tree. Trees in the Polish (Slavic) Folklore and Culture: Part 1." *Lamus Dworski*, 19 Mar. 2017, https://lamusdworski.wordpress.com/2017/03/19/linden-tree/.

Lin, Jian, et al. "Socioeconomic and spatial inequalities of street tree abundance, species diversity, and size structure in New York City." *Landscape and Urban Planning*, vol. 206, 2021, p. 103992, https://doi.org/10.1016/j.landurbplan.2020.103992.

Malgorzata Blicharska, Richard J. Smithers, Białowieża Forest: Political stands. *Science* 359, 646-646(2018). DOI:10.1126/science.aar7173

McDonald RI, Biswas T, Sachar C, Housman I, Boucher TM, Balk D, et al. (2021) The tree cover and temperature disparity in US urbanized areas: Quantifying the association with income across 5,723 communities. PLoS ONE 16(4): e0249715. https://doi.org/10.1371/journal.pone.0249715

Meldon, Perri. "Harriet Tubman Underground Railroad State Park." *American Quarterly*, vol. 72 no. 4, 2020, p. 979-991. *Project MUSE*, doi:10.1353/aq.2020.0055.

Pascal et Thierry. "Le Tilleul de Sully." *Petit-Patrimoine.com*, 2015, www.petit-patrimoine.com/fiche-petit-patrimoine.php?id_pp=89044_4.

"Plantation d'Arbres Le 14 Juillet 1989 Dans Les Communes." *Sénat*, 9 Feb. 1989, www.senat.fr/questions/base/1989/qSEQ890203452.html.

"Poland." *World Sensorium / Conservancy*, 17 Oct. 2022, worldsensorium.com/poland/.

Powers, Richard. *The Overstory*. W.W. Norton & Company, 2018.

Tenche-Constantinescu, A. M., et al. "The symbolism of the linden tree." *Journal of Horticulture, Forestry and Biotechnology* 19.2 (2015): 237-242.

Thompson, Jonathan R., et al. "Four Centuries of Change in Northeastern United States Forests." PLOS ONE, vol. 8, no. 9, Public Library of Science, Sept. 2013, pp. e72540-40, https://doi.org/10.1371/journal.pone.0072540.

"Tilia Americana L." *Native American Ethnobotany Database*, naeb.brit.org/uses/species/3959/.

"Topography of the Camp." *Muzeum Treblinka*, muzeumtreblinka.eu/en/informacje/topography-of-the-camp/.

World, UNESCO. "Białowieża Forest." *Unesco.org*, 2018, whc.unesco.org/en/list/33/.

THIS SONG IS A COVER

BARR, "This Song is A Cover", Beyond Reinforced Jewel Case, 5RC 2005. MP3/CD

Farfán-Heredia, B., Casas, A. & Rangel-Landa, S. Cultural, economic, and ecological factors influencing management of wild plants and mushrooms interchanged in Purépecha markets of Mexico. *J Ethnobiology Ethnomedicine* 14, 68 (2018). https://doi.org/10.1186/s13002-018-0269-9

Hanrahan, Clare, and Rebecca J. Frey, PhD. "Pennyroyal." *The Gale Encyclopedia of Alternative Medicine*, edited by Deirdre S. Hiam, 5th ed., vol. 4, Gale, 2020, pp. 2054-2057. *Gale eBooks*, link.gale.com/apps/doc/CX7947800671/GVRL?u=upenn_main&sid=summon&xid=3c00c6bc

"Pliny the Elder, the Natural History, BOOK XX. REMEDIES DERIVED from the GARDEN PLANTS., CHAP. 54.—PENNYROYAL: TWENTY-FIVE REMEDIES." *Tufts.edu*, 2023, www.perseus.tufts.edu/hopper/text?doc=Perseus%3Atext%3A1999.02.0137%3Abook%3D20%3Achapter%3D54.

Smith, C. Earle, and Ellen Messer. *The Vegetational History of the Oaxaca Valley and Zapotec Plant Knowledge*. E-book, Ann Arbor, MI: University of Michigan Museum of Anthropological Archaeology, 1978, https://doi.org/10.3998/mpub.11396149.

Turner, B. L. "Taxonomic status of Clinopodium macrostemum (Lamiaceae)." *Phytologia* 90.3 (2008): 411-413. https://biostor.org/reference/208564

Viveros-Valdez, Ezequiel et al. "Antiproliferative effect from the Mexican poleo (Hedeoma drummondii)." *Journal of medicinal food* vol. 13,3 (2010): 740-2. doi:10.1089/jmf.2009.0041

Kanye West. "Monster". My Dark Twisted Fantasy. Def Jam Recordings. 2010. MP3

Arendt, Hannah and Scholem, Gershom. "Part one: The letters". *The Correspondence of Hannah Arendt and Gershom Scholem*, edited by Marie Luise Knott, Chicago: University of Chicago Press, 2017

Belle and Sebastian. "Get Me Away from Here I'm Dying". If You're Feeling Sinister, Jeepster Records, 1996. CD

Benjamin, Walter, et al. "A Berlin Chronicle." *One-Way Street*, The Belknap Press of Harvard University Press, Cambridge, MA, 2016

Benjamin, Walter. *The Arcades Project*. First Harvard University Press paperback edition. Cambridge, Mass.: Belknap Press of Harvard University Press, 2002

Benjamin Walter. *L'œuvre D'art À L'epoque De Sa Reproductibilité Technique*. Éd. Allia 2003.

Brook, James. "Remarks on the Poetic Transformation of San Francisco." *Reclaiming San Francisco: History, Politics, Culture: A City Lights Anthology*, edited by James Brook et al., City Lights, San Francisco, CA, 1998

"Even the Dead Won't Be Safe': Walter Benjamin's Final Journey | the National WWII Museum | New Orleans." *The National WWII Museum | New Orleans*, 30 Sept. 2020, www.nationalww2museum.org/war/articles/walter-benjamin.

Hill, Samantha Rose. "Walter Benjamin's Last Work." *Los Angeles Review of Books*, 9 Dec. 2019, https://lareviewofbooks.org/article/walter-benjamins-last-work/.

Julie Doiron. "Sweeter." Loneliest in the Morning. Jagjaguwar,1997. MP3

MacCannell, Dean. *The Tourist: a New Theory of the Leisure Class*. New York: Schocken Books, 1976
Saletti, Carlo, and Véronique Lippmann. "Le souvenir de Walter Benjamin à Port-Brou (Espagne)." *Revue d'histoire de la Shoah* 2 (2004): 225-230.

Sorgue, Pierre. "Sur Les Traces de Walter Benjamin." *Le Monde.fr*, Le Monde, 10 Sept. 2021, www.lemonde.fr/m-styles/article/2021/09/10/sur-les-traces-de-walter-benjamin_6094223_4497319.html.

Suicide. "Johnny." *Suicide*. Red Star Records, 1977. MP3

Talking Heads "(Nothing But) Flowers", Naked. Sire, 1988. MP3

The Fates. "No Romance". Furia. Taboo Records, 1985. MP3

The Mae Shi. "Power to the Power/Bite Two".Terrorbird, 5 Rue Christine, 2004. MP3

HEAVENLY TREE

"Ailanthus Altissima." *Plants of Louisiana*, US Geological Survey, warcapps.usgs.gov/PlantID/Species/Details/2029. Accessed 2 Oct. 2022.

DePuy, LeRoy B. "The Walnut Street prison: Pennsylvania's first penitentiary." *Pennsylvania History: A Journal of Mid-Atlantic Studies* 18.2 (1951): 130-144.

Field Guide for Managing Tree-of-heaven in the Southwest. Revised May 2017. Albuquerque, NM: United States Department of Agriculture, Forest Service, Southwestern Region, 2017.

Fryer, Janet L. 2010. Ailanthus altissima. In: Fire Effects Information System,

[Online]. U.S. Department of Agriculture, Forest Service, Rocky Mountain Research Station, Fire Sciences Laboratory (Producer). Available: https://www.fs.usda.gov/database/feis/plants/tree/ailalt/all.html.

Gómez-Aparicio, Lorena, and Charles D. Canham. "Neighbourhood Analyses of the Allelopathic Effects of the Invasive Tree Ailanthus Altissima in Temperate Forests." Journal of Ecology 96, no. 3 (2008): 447–58. http://www.jstor.org/stable/20143483.

Heisey, Rod M. "Allelopathy and the Secret Life of Ailanthus Altissima." Arnoldia 57, no. 3 (1997): 28–36. http://www.jstor.org/stable/42954526.

Hu, Shiu Ying. "Ailanthus." Arnoldia 39, no. 2 (1979): 29–50. http://www.jstor.org/stable/42954660.

Lawrence, Jeffrey G., Alison Colwell, and Owen J. Sexton. "The Ecological Impact of Allelopathy in Ailanthus Altissima (Simaroubaceae)." American Journal of Botany 78, no. 7 (1991): 948–58. https://doi.org/10.2307/2445173.

Li, Xiang & Li, Yao & Ma, Shanbo & Zhao, Qianqian & Wu, Junsheng & Duan, Linrui & Xie, Yanhua & Wang, Siwang. (2021). Traditional uses, phytochemistry, and pharmacology of Ailanthus altissima (Mill.) Swingle bark: A comprehensive review. Journal of ethnopharmacology. 275. 114121. 10.1016/j.jep.2021.114121.

Nilsen, Erik T., Cynthia D. Huebner, David E. Carr, and Zhe Bao. 2018. "Interaction between Ailanthus altissima and Native Robinia pseudoacacia in Early Succession: Implications for Forest Management" Forests 9, no. 4: 221. https://doi.org/10.3390/f9040221

Nowak, David J.; Bodine, Allison R.; Hoehn III, Robert E.; Ellis, Alexis; Low, Sarah C.; Roman, Lara A.; Henning, Jason G.; Stephan, Emily; Taggert, Tom; Endreny, Ted. 2016. The urban forests of Philadelphia. Resource Bulletin NRS-106. Newtown Square, PA: U.S. Department of Agriculture, Forest Service, Northern Research Station. 80 p.

Patrick, Darren. "Queering the Urban Forest: Invasions, Mutualisms, and Eco-Political Creativity with the Tree of Heaven (Ailanthus altissima)." (2014).

Shah, Behula. "The Checkered Career of Ailanthus Altissima." Arnoldia 57, no. 3 (1997): 20–27. http://www.jstor.org/stable/42954525.

Sladonja, B., Sušek, M. & Guillermic, J. Review on Invasive Tree of Heaven (Ailanthus altissima (Mill.) Swingle) Conflicting Values: Assessment of Its Ecosystem Services and Potential Biological Threat. Environmental Management 56, 1009–1034 (2015). https://doi.org/10.1007/s00267-015-0546-5

Swingle, Walter T. "The Early European History and the Botanical Name of the Tree of Heaven, Ailanthus Altissima." Journal of the Washington Academy of Sciences 6, no. 14 (1916): 490–98. http://www.jstor.org/stable/24521283.

The Farm: Angola USA, produced and directed by Jonathan Stack, Liz Garbus ; A film by Gabriel Films; Funded by A&E Network. The Farm: Angola USA. [New York, NY]: Gabriel Films, 1998.(https://warcapps.usgs.gov/PlantID/Species/Details/2029)

Wang R, Lu Y, Li H, et al. Antitumor activity of the Ailanthus altissima bark phytochemical ailanthone against breast cancer MCF-7 cells. Oncol Lett. 2018;15(4):6022-6028. doi:10.3892/ol.2018.8039

Woodfox, Albert. Solitary: *Unbroken by four decades in solitary confinement. My story of transformation and hope.* Grove Press, 2019.

Cech Richo and Sena Cech. *Making Plant Medicine.* Fourth ed. Herbal Reads 2016.

Cohen, Deatra, and Adam Siegel. *Ashkenazi Herbalism: Rediscovering the Herbal Traditions of Eastern European Jews.* North Atlantic Books, 2021.

Davis, Mike. *Magical Urbanism: Latinos Reinvent the US City.* Verso, 2000.

Dixon Ejeris and Leah Lakshmi Piepzna-Samarasinha. *Beyond Survival: Strategies and Stories from the Transformative Justice Movement.* AK Press 2020.

Feghali, Layla. "What Does 'Plantcestor' Mean?" *Ancestral HUB | reCollecting Our Stories Home,* 21 Apr. 2016, swanaancestralmedicinehub.wordpress.com/2015/03/11/what-does-plantcestor-mean/.

FEGHALI LAYLA. *Land in Our Bones: Plantcestral Herbalism and Healing Cultures from Syria to the Sinai -... Earth-Based Pathways to Ancestral Stewardship And.* NORTH ATLANTIC BOOKS 2024.

Gilmore Ruth Wilson. *Golden Gulag : Prisons Surplus Crisis and Opposition in Globalizing California.* University of California Press 2007.

Haines, Staci. *The Politics of Trauma: Somatics Healing and Social Justice.* North Atlantic Books 2019.

Imarisha, Walidah. *Angels with Dirty Faces: Three Stories of Crime Prison and Redemption.* AK Press 2016.

Kaba Mariame et al. *We Do This 'Til We Free Us: Abolitionist Organizing and Transforming Justice.* Haymarket Books 2021.

Kimmerer, Robin W. *Braiding Sweetgrass.* Milkweed Editions, 2020.

Levine Peter A and Maggie Kline. *Trauma through a Child's Eyes: Awakening the Ordinary Miracle of Healing*. North Atlantic Books 2006.

Menakem, Resmaa. *My Grandmother's Hands Racialized Trauma and the Pathway to Mending Our Hearts and Bodies*. Central Recovery Press 2017.

Ndefo, Nkem. "The Body as Compass." *FOR the WILD podcast*, 24 Mar. 2021, forthewild.world/listen/nkem-ndefo-on-the-body-as-compass-227.

Perry Bruce D and Maia Szalavitz. *The Boy Who Was Raised As a Dog*. Basic Books 2017.

Said, Edward W. *Orientalism*. Penguin Books 1995.

Thom, Kai Cheng. *I Hope We Choose Love: A Trans Girl's Notes from the End of the World*. Arsenal Pulp Press 2019.

Photo Credit: Shoog McDaniel — shoogmcdaniel.com

NOAM KEIM (they/them) is a trauma worker, medicine maker and flâneur freak. Their non-fiction writing weaves themes close to their heart: reverence to the land, healing, queerness, colonialism, plants, abolition. They are a Lambda Literary '22 Fellow, an RWW '23 Fellow, a Tin House '23 Fellow, a Sewanee '23 contributor and a Periplus '23 Fellow mentored by Grace Talusan. Connect on Twitter and IG at thelandisholy or thelandisholy.com.

About the Publisher

RADIX is a worker-owned, union printer and publisher based in Brooklyn, New York. They publish fresh perspectives, prioritizing the voices of typically marginalized communities. Their name comes from the Latin root of the word *radical*, meaning to get to the root.

Their books have won awards from *Foreword Reviews* and AIGA.

Colophon

At Radix, we pride ourselves in owning the means of production, and in crafting books that will give the reader joy from the moment the book is in their hands.

We printed this book on 70# Mohswk Via Vellum text stock with union labor in Brooklyn, New York, using an AB Dick 9995 offset press.

The cover was letterpress printed in two-colors on 100# cover stock, using a Heidelberg Windmill, a press that exudes timelessness and quality.

Other Titles by Radix

We Are Many: Defending Women & Sex Worker Human Rights
Anthology, ed. Beldan Sezen & Adam Shapiro

Many Worlds, Or The Simulacra
Anthology, ed. Cadwell Turnbull & Josh Eure

Is This How You Eat a Watermelon?
Zein El-Amine

Mortals
John Dermot Woods & Matt L.

Fanning the Flames: A Molly Crabapple Coloring Book
Molly Crabapple

The Solar Grid
Ganzeer

There Is Still Singing in the Afterlife
JinJin Xiu

BINT
Ghinwa Jawhari

We Are All Things
Elliott Colla & Ganzeer

Futures: A Science Fiction Series
Various

Be the Change! A Justseeds Coloring Book
Justseeds Artists' Cooperative, ed. Molly Fair

Aftermath: Explorations of Loss & Grief
Anthology, ed. Radix Media